TALISMAN

TALISMAN

Global Positioning
for the Soul

Tom Bandy

CHALICE
PRESS

ST. LOUIS, MISSOURI

Cover art: Getty Images
Cover and interior design: Elizabeth Wright

Visit Chalice Press on the World Wide Web at
www.chalicepress.com

10 9 8 7 6 5 4 3 2 1   06 07 08 09 10 11

Library of Congress Cataloging–in–Publication Data

Bandy, Thomas G., 1950-
  Talisman : global positioning for the soul / T.G. Bandy.
    p. cm.
  Includes bibliographical references.
  ISBN-13: 978-0-8272-3648-6 (pbk.)
  ISBN-10: 0-8272-3648-4 (pbk.)
  1. Spiritual life—Christianity. I. Title.
  BV4501.3.B356 2006
  248.4—dc22

                                                   2005037544

Printed in the United States of America

Contents

Forward

My name is Echo. It is my network name, of course, but it is also my nickname. I was named for my generation by parents who were at a loss with what to do with me and unconfident of any future worth inheriting.

My great-grandparents were "Silents" who said little, repressed their anger, indulged their children, and burdened my parents with the future. They gave their children stalwart, traditional names like "William" and "Mary," hoping the past would be safe in their memories.

My grandparents were "Boomers" who primarily valued the past for what they could possess and sell on the Antiques Roadshow. They were the most selfish generation the world has ever known, proclaiming peace, relishing intimacy, and destroying the environment to feed an insatiable need for golf courses and comfortable homes. They gave their children names like "Storm" and "Flower," hoping they could live vicariously through the achievements of their children.

My parents (all five of them) were "Busters." In addition to two natural parents (one of whom I have never seen), I have two stepfathers and a "significant other" that my most recent stepfather has been living with ever since my mother died of breast cancer. What they lacked in continuity they made up for in portability as they moved from place to place and relationship to relationship, questing for the elusive career, healing balm, and lottery win. They gave me and my various brothers and sisters, stepbrothers and stepsisters, and illegitimate brothers and sisters names like "Dirk" and "Ashley," hoping that our romantic lives would make their dreams concrete.

My generation has decided not to accept the gift of a name. We create our own. I suppose our intention is to express our radical individuality, but I suspect it is also a convenient way to protect our anonymity. We have been abused way too much and are cautious about self-revelations. We really are an echo of the urgent whispers, boasting shouts, and inarticulate stammers vocalized by previous generations in the heat of the day and the dark of the night.

Culture is a bit hollow to us. It is like a vast museum with cavernous hallways of memorabilia and aspirations, in which the sounds of our footsteps reverberate. We are neither lost nor found, just bouncing. We are neither contented nor rebellious, just curious. We are neither happy nor depressed, just experimenting. We are disembodied spirits looking for a way out from the "hall of science and technology" and from the "portrait gallery of great leaders" and from the "evolutionary history of planet earth" and from the ever-present ticket counters and the ever-silent museum ushers who move us along, tell us to be quiet, and caution us against touching any sacred artifacts.

My name is Echo, and therefore I cannot speak for my generation with the same confidence with which my ancestors spoke for their generations. I'm not even sure I can speak for myself, consistently, from one year to the next. I play all kinds of music, in vinyl recordings on my old-fashioned turntable. I have given up Web sites for blogs, e-mail for instant messaging, any form of communication with wires attached, and any form of relationship with strings attached. I learned to fly when I was young, but so far I have not bothered to learn to drive. I appreciate trends, but I personally have no fashion sense whatsoever.

Chameleon-like, I can look, talk, work, and act like any of my previous generations. Dress me in a suit, and I can be effective at the bank. Dress me in chinos, and I can sell anything at the mall. I will be the next business leader, health care provider, social service administrator, and public school principle; but it will still be a veneer. I quest for authenticity, but am not sure I would recognize it if I saw it.

That is, until now. I first met Mentor as a guest lecturer at the community college and subsequently followed him through Web sites, churches, synagogues, university student unions, social service networks, and other distinctly odd places where he gathered with his disciples. This is simply a sampling of what he said, and I am not sure where and in what order he said it. He introduced us to a different kind of spiritual discipline, taught us a different kind of partnered journaling, and unlocked a door out of the cultural museum in which we lived.

That is why I introduce this record with a "Forward" rather than a "Foreword." My pilgrim band has no intention of going back into the museum. Spirit has intersected with culture; and whether life is on-the-edge, in-between, or at-peace, it will never be the same. Occasionally I have included excerpts from my journal, but mainly I have collected the essential wisdom that gave us hope and purpose.

Echo
200 B.C.E.—2006 C.E.

Keywords

Learning the Language of Global Positioning for the Soul

The Language of Intersection

the infinite—Boundless, endless, ultimate, unconditioned perfection
the finite—Limited, aging, temporary, conditional existence
the eternal now—The moment of timeless fulfillment

Telos—The purposeful culmination of time and space
Kairos—Unexpected moments of decisive change
Mythos—Meaningful interpretations or reenactments of divine purpose
Logos—The fundamental structure of reason and reality
Chronos—The moment-to-moment passage of time

the power of being—The vitality, dynamism, creativity, and passion of life
the depth of being—The stability, predictability, inevitability, and significance of life
ultimate concern—The absolute, unconditioned claim on one's loyalty and life

The Language of Incarnation

Christ the New Being—Experiences of incarnation that shatter and shape life
Christ the Vindicator—Experiences of incarnation that defeat evil and establish good
Christ the Perfect Human—Experiences of incarnation that reveal human potential and hope

Jesus the Promise Keeper—Experiences of incarnation that guarantee fidelity and redemption
Jesus the Healer—Experiences of incarnation that restore complete health
Jesus the Spiritual Guide—Experiences of incarnation that mentor through the ambiguities of life

Eros—Desire for reunion, passion for creativity, imagination for
  innovation
Agape—Surrender of self for the good of another
Phileos—Friendship, loyalty, and accountability among others on a
  shared journey

The Language of Journaling

infinite beginnings—Fresh starts caused by the unexpected initiative of
  God (see *Kairos*)
meaning patterns—Human interpretations of the significance of history
  (see *Mythos*)
reasonable order—Predictable, logical expectations of mind and nature
  (see *Logos*)

intimate beginnings—Fresh starts caused by deep and significant human
  relationships
life struggles—Trial and error in the daily challenge to survive and
  thrive
spiritual coaching—Mentoring and training for wise decisions and
  moral actions

life-on-the-edge—High risk living that changes the status quo and
  explores the unknown
life-in-between—Tentative living that endures ambiguity and questions
  next steps
life-at-peace—Serene living that enjoys fulfillment and rests on
  accomplishment

oppositions—Locating your life between the extreme poles of life in the
  spirit (life-on-the-edge)
juxtapositions—Locating your life between adjacent points of infinite
  meaning (life-in-between)
acceptance—Locating your life in the continuity between lifestyle and
  destiny (life-at-peace)

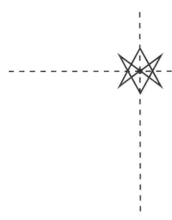

Talisman Touch

Revealing the Power of Being

There is more here than meets the mind. Before the printing press, public education, and university diplomas, the ancients knew that "Being" would always surpass our efforts to control it. The Beautiful would always surpass our best works of art. The Good would always challenge our best acts of morality. The True would always extend beyond our best articulations of religion and philosophy. They knew. There would always be a depth of being that would make reason, justice, and creativity *possible* and *insufficient* at the same time.

This intuition of the ancients was more revelation than deduction. This same intuition is emerging today as the Age of Reason reaches the limits of adequacy to guide the enterprise of living. What is the contemporary explosion of music—in all forms, in all places, at all times—if not a rebellion against scientific rationalism? What is the expansion of the Internet if not an admission of the inadequacy of controlling reason? What is the proliferation of image and visual art—sprayed on urban walls, emblazoned on clothing, or burned into the flesh—if not a celebration that there is *more* to life than the passage of time? There must be more. There is an ultimate concern that is at once beautiful, good, and true. The ancients would have understood. As the modern world passes away, so also do the learning methodologies and the personal growth goals of people in search of a God beyond all gods.

Witness the reemergence of the "talisman." A talisman functions as a "Global Positioning System" for the soul. It is both symbol and portal. It is symbol in the sense that it bids the mind recall essential truths about life and death, God and destiny. It is portal in the sense that it opens a momentary and ill-defined conduit between infinite meaning and any particular human heart. As symbol, the talisman analyzes and illuminates, helping an individual exclaim, "Now I see!" As portal, the talisman synthesizes and strengthens, helping an individual exclaim, "Now I shall endure!"

Any data byte can become a talisman: an image, a sound, a song, a movement, or an object. Yet because the talisman is both symbol *and* portal, an individual never quite chooses the talisman. The talisman chooses the individual. No talisman is forever. Only the infinite is forever. The infinite may reach out to seize a data byte and force itself upon an individual's attention. An individual might select a talisman and coax the infinite to fill it with meaning. Yet the infinite will eventually reject the talisman as essentially limited and incapable of conveying the fullness of infinity (the Beautiful, the Good, and the True).

The talisman may be a relic of antiquity or an expression of radical originality. It may be a stone from the beach, a tattoo on the flesh, a photo, a sculpture, a rhythm, a dance, a verse, or a phrase. If it is a "word,"

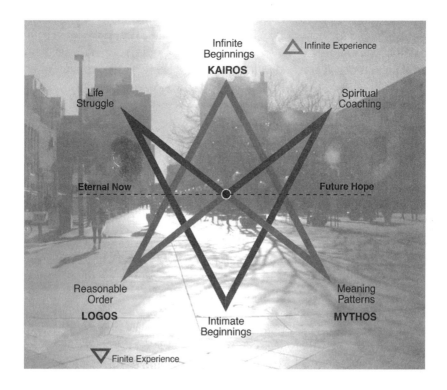

it is not an essay. It is poetry, metaphor, reflection in a mirror, and a face perceived in a dream. It is not "words" but "Word," a creative utterance that elicits a change of habit, a redirection of attitude, and a surge of hope.

Every talisman has an "inner nature," and that is what I have tried to capture in this book. This inner nature of a talisman is like the "fire" inside a diamond. Our talisman is a six-pointed star. Formed by the intersection of the finite and the infinite, this star becomes a kind of "map" for the pilgrim journey of every human being. Any image can be placed underneath the star diagram, and the star diagram can lead you to explore the significance of any image. Meditation on whatever talisman has seized your imagination leads you into this inner map that can help you chart your course and anticipate your next step in the quest for God. You can create a digital "talisman" unique to your personal spirituality with images available on www.easumbandy.com.

The six-pointed star is formed by the intersection of the infinite reaching down into our existence and the finite reaching out toward ultimate concern for the Beautiful, the Good, and the True. The talisman is both an incarnation and a pointer toward many incarnations, in which the fullness of the absolute momentarily fills our limited existence.

Talismans render the infinite *predictable.* Therefore, the infinite, which is essentially uncontrollable, will eventually shatter the talisman. If an individual has elevated the talisman to ultimate concern (a common form of idolatry frequent in pagan worlds), then the infinite will shatter the individual along with it. Yet if a person handles the talisman rightly, then the individual can use the talisman to gain both insight and courage for life. When the infinite shatters the talisman, the individual can continue to thrive in the spiritual discipline that the talisman has empowered. That discipline will in turn open the individual to a new talisman—a new image, sound, movement, or object—which will in its uniqueness affirm and challenge, encourage and disturb, and goad the individual deeper into the spiritual life. The desire of the finite to render the infinite predictable precipitates an eternal struggle, for the infinite demands of the finite unrelenting growth.

How does one find a talisman—or, more accurately, how does one allow a talisman to find him or her? The answer is to engage the spiritual discipline implied by any and all talismans. Fundamentally, this involves a surrender of individual "control" over activities, relationships, and even ideas. Management, manipulation, and dogmatism must be systematically and courageously "pared away" from one's lifestyle. Replace "control" with "purposefulness" or the sheer desire for unity with the infinite.

Such "desire for God," as the ancient monastic mentors might call it, relinquishes control over life. It simplifies activities, reducing the need for luxury. It focuses on the well-being of others, reducing the need for approval. It focuses on the import that lies behind idea, reducing the need for rational certainty. The more the individual pares away control for purposefulness, the more likely that person will be to discover, or be discovered by, talisman. Existential choice will always be surpassed by infinite import, and the temporary result of that interaction will be an ever-expanding depth of meaning.

Therefore, in addition to the star diagram that illustrates the inner nature of any talisman, I also introduce you to an ancient and reapplied discipline of spiritual growth and accountability. Various religions and spiritualities have used "prayer beads" as a talisman and spiritual discipline all in one. Christians of all kinds have used the rosary, but I have sought to redefine it and adapt it to the Global Positioning System that is the inner nature of every talisman. The "Hope Rosary," as I have come to call it, is a discipline among pilgrim companions to align their lives with divine purpose and merge their lifestyles in infinite meaning.

This book is aimed at three of the five generations of the "legion of the lapsed" (former participants in institutional religion who have dropped out, opted out, and are looking for more). It is for the "rationally reserved," the "seriously experimenting," and the "radically committed." It is not really for the "spiritual dilettantes" or the "flaky fringe." My debt to my mentor Paul Tillich and to an attitude toward life extending from Plato, Origen, Antony, and Augustine through Boehme, Bergson, Schelling, Unamuno, and on through mystics from many places and times will be obvious to the more philosophically inclined.

Mentors pass their insights to their disciples and trust that, in the right time, they can sort out the very profound from the really stupid. The real gift of the mentor, however, is passion for the quest. This book is really told through the hearing of my ideal disciple, Echo, whose questions follow me wherever I go. I have invited him to close with a few words of encouragement to read on…

The key question is this. Do you desire God? *Do you yearn for the infinite? Do you ache to feel the touch of the Holy? Do you want to taste it, touch it, smell the scent of it, hear the whisper, see the reality, and experience the presence? This book is for lovers longing for a glimpse of the Beloved and daring to believe that the Beloved is searching for them.*

PART 1

Global Positioning for the Soul

The Legion of the Lapsed

The fastest growing demographic in the world (and especially in North America, Western Europe, Great Britain, and Australia) is the spiritually yearning, institutionally alienated public. These are the legion of the lapsed—formerly of one religious institution or another—now distancing themselves consciously or unconsciously from their institutionally religious past. Yet they are profoundly, and increasingly, interested in spiritual things. They are convinced that there is an elusive wholeness to life that beckons to them from somewhere. This sought-for, longed-for wholeness includes relational, intellectual, emotional, physical, and, yes, spiritual health. This legion of the lapsed are also convinced that there is a depth of meaning and purpose—a Logos and Telos—that lies tantalizingly just beyond the reach of human creativity. This legion of the lapsed have lost their bearings in the expanding universe, and they are urgently seeking to discern where they are and where they might yet go.

Who are they? They are generally well educated, graduates of secondary schooling and probably with at least basic university education. They have been raised as children of the Enlightenment, products of both the Industrial and Technology Revolutions, trained in the principles of pragmatism and the methods of science. They are convinced that truth should be rational, manageable, controllable, and therapeutic. They are intelligent, creative, fair minded, compassionate, and imminently reasonable people—but they live in a chronic state of anxiety and disillusionment as they watch intelligence, fairness, compassion, and reason erode in the midst of life and as they fail despite their best efforts.

For example, over here are the doctors, nurses, or health care professionals. Educated in the sciences and trained in the latest technologies, they have a keen sense of holistic health. Perhaps they grew up in the Roman Catholic Church. They remain highly influenced by the sacramental and caring ministries of its parishes, orders, and institutions. They are inspired by memories of Saint Francis and Mother Teresa. They are convinced that spiritual discipline, applied reason, faith in God, and flexible institutional understanding can combine to improve health and moral integrity.

Only it hasn't worked. They watch their hospitals and nursing homes being downsized, the church becoming increasingly intolerant in the face of radical diversity, and the health care system being treated as a political football among politicians, pharmaceutical researchers, and insurance companies. Occasionally they still go to mass, but increasingly it does not satisfy the intuition and craving that there is something deeper, more compelling, and more hopeful than rites, liturgies, and authoritative pronouncements.

Over there are the teachers, professors, or public school administrators. Educated in the liberal arts, trained in the most up-to-date learning methodologies, they understand the difference between a vocation and a job. Perhaps they grew up in a Protestant denomination and are still highly influenced by both the Protestant work ethic and Protestant justice. Inspired by memories of Martin Luther King, Jr., and Nelson Mandela, they stand convinced that knowledge, informed choices, and a little help from an enlightened government can combine to overcome racism, poverty, and crime.

Only it hasn't worked. They watch their urban schools crumble, their suburban schools obsess over relative trivialities, and their school boards pay more attention to pensions than to life change. Occasionally they still go to church, but increasingly it does not satisfy the itch, the yearning and the questioning that there must be something more hopeful than polities, sermons, and protests.

Out there are the corporate men and women of business—perhaps a small business entrepreneur or a senior management professional. Educated in business, with extra specialization in law or human resources or logistics, they already know that corporate ideology and personal spirituality have merged in the workplace. They grew up in any of a number of religious institutions (Christian, Jewish, Muslim, and more) and are still connected with any number of philanthropic foundations with religious roots. Innovative inventors and corporate giants inspire them, but so do social crusaders and political revolutionaries. They are convinced that the "power of one" and the "power of we" can be harnessed both to make a profit and to improve the quality of life and general peace in the global neighborhood.

Only it hasn't worked. They watch their companies being gobbled up by profiteering multinationals, unions slowing down the pace of change, governments taxing away the income originally targeted for research and development, and colleagues investing more in fast cars and golf memberships than in marriage enrichment and family life. Occasionally they still go to church, synagogue, mosque, or temple and hold still long enough for prayer. But increasingly it does not satisfy the longing for something more hopeful than heritage preservation and public policies.

Finally, here are the social service workers or nonprofit CEOs. Educated in psychology, sociology, and the arts—very possibly a seminary graduate—they are simultaneously committed to a cause and passionately in love with a microculture. They grew up in churches, parachurches, or other faith-based institutions, often to an advanced level of initiation. They gain inspiration from many sources: the Renaissance; every revolution from Arthurian legend straight through the struggles of America, France, Russia, and Vietnam; the unionization of the railroads; and the civil rights movements for blacks, women, and any group that is in any way downtrodden or oppressed or underprivileged. They are convinced that a creative combination of consciousness raising, affirmative action, radical education, and modest government intervention can eventually create a just, clean, peaceful society.

Only it hasn't worked. They watch policies shifting with the political winds, funding being wasted or inconsistently applied, and three new pockets of oppression replacing every one that has been removed. Occasionally they still go to church or attend the alumni gathering of their college or seminary, but increasingly it does not satisfy the dream of something more hopeful than another strategic plan.

These people, and many more, are among the legion of the lapsed. Certainly they are "lapsed" from their former religious loyalties, but also they are "lapsed" from the idealism, passion, and clarity of purpose that motivated their first ventures into education, health care, business, and social service. This legion of the lapsed have lost their bearings in the expanding universe, and they are urgently seeking to discern where they are and where they might yet go.

Just as a compass was calibrated to true north, so also leaders in education, health care, business, and social service have an internal compass set by the eternal truth and absolute principles advocated and interpreted by the religious institutions of their past. As the credibility and general trustworthiness of those institutions have eroded, so also their advocacy and interpretation of basic principles of life and meaning no longer guide the heart and imagination of the individual leader. Eventually all institutional advocacy and all interpretation are treated with such cynicism that truth itself is doubted. It is as if the North Star has been obscured by so much, for so long, that its existence itself becomes the stuff of dreams alone.

Nor can confidence in truth be restored simply by renewing the credibility of the old institutions. Once lost, confidence is rarely regained, unless something truly radical happens to those institutions. That is only going to happen by ceasing to tinker with the institutions and seeking instead the real source of meaning and purpose. My experience with religious institutions is that they are stubborn, intransigent things. No amount of coaxing will move them to recalibrate themselves. The heart must first fly to the truth. Either the old mythologies will be renewed and the old institutions will adjust or the heart of the seeker will invent new mythologies and design new institutions for the future.

Each decade brings acceleration to both the degree of alienation and the degree of yearning. In the 1970s, media interest focused on claims that ancient Christianity and Judaism were really institutional subterfuges for cults of sacred mushrooms. It was all sparked by fringe interpretations of the Dead Sea Scrolls and renewed interest in ancient mystery cults.

In the 1980s, media interest focused on New Age movements, crystals, and Kabala. It was all sparked by spiritual mentors to "famous people" and environmental concerns.

In the 1990s, media interest focused on the Jesus Seminar and a new quest for historical accuracy that reduced the reliability of the Bible to a mere handful of verses. This was sparked by maverick academic scholars and publishing house marketing.

At the moment, media interest focuses on the *Da Vinci Code,* fueled by the unveiling of archeological hoaxes and the suspicion that a centuries-old conspiracy has kept the public in the dark about the real truth about Jesus. The "North American Religions" and "New Religious Movement" sections of the American Academy of Religion have grown exponentially in just three decades.

There is a parallel between the increasing popularity of media attention to religious and supernatural themes over the past several decades ("May the Force be with you!" and "The truth is out there!") and the steady decline of established religious organizations. It is noteworthy that none of these outbreaks of spiritual interest last for long. They dominate the media for a time and then seem to vanish from the consciousness of the public overnight. It is even more noteworthy that these outbreaks of spiritual zealotry are increasing in frequency and passion.

ECHO'S JOURNAL _

Today I heard a remarkable speech at the grand opening of a new mental health center that put into words the intuition that has been nagging at me for some time. The rational world is not enough. The manageable, controllable, understandable, witty, charming, cynical, sarcastic, ironic, and consumer world that powerfully motivate me to linger at Starbucks is not enough. CNN, reality TV, and the sports channels are not enough. Philanthropic service, political advocacy, and the Internet are not enough. There's got to be more of a point to life than I have yet found. And it is out there waiting to be discovered.

No, that's not quite right. I am in here, waiting for "it" to discover me. Or maybe it is both/and.

The speech crystallized in my mind the reason I have this approach-avoidance relationship with my ancestors. I seem to select odd bits of influence from my parents, grandparents, and great-grandparents—the generations that preceded me—and leave large chunks behind. I am a "lapsed" Catholic-Protestant-Buddhist-techno/scientific-humanistic-adult juvenile delinquent—who is now teaching others what I only partly believe, leading programs in which I have only partial confidence, and doing business with only half-hearted enthusiasm.

It's not just that there is something wrong with the world. There is something odd about me and my colleagues. We are "lapsed." At some point at the turn of millennium the warranty ran out guaranteeing replacement parts for modernity, and we are on our own.

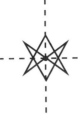

The Ancient Awe

First-century Christians and Jews would have described the legion of the lapsed as "God-Fearers." Then, as now, the lapsed public included refugees from all the institutional religions and philosophies of the time. Among them were *former* adherents in the various temples of Jupiter, Artemis, Athena, and more; *former* participants in the cults of Isis, Orpheus, Roma, and more; and *former* Stoics, Epicureans, Platonists, and more. Politics, tradition, and lingering superstition kept these lapsed "God-Fearers" loosely tied to the home religion. Attendance at Saturnalia or Christmas would go up if only for good luck, family harmony, and a chance to get out of the house to party. But the old institutions and disciplines had lost their deeper sense of the Holy, and these ancient God-Fearers searched elsewhere and everywhere to find it.

The ancient awe they sought certainly predated the first century. This is one reason why religions from Judea, Persia, and Egypt became so popular. The God-Fearers were eager for the immediacy of the Holy. They grew impatient with any institutional mediation. They longed to be swept away, transformed, connected, and enlightened—and were prepared to risk hurt for the sake of the ecstasy, suffer divorce for the sake of true intimacy, and sacrifice career for the sake of personal destiny. Sound familiar?

Whether they believed in one God or many gods—and whether this God or these gods were alternatively lumps of carved stone, persons, or spirits—was really *not* their main concern. They cared about how humanity in general, and themselves in particular, fit into the great ladder of being.

What was their place, their purpose, their role in the larger destiny of the universe? Certain themes from all the ancient religions captured their imagination:

• **The cycle of birth, death, resurrection, and new life:** Death has a greater meaning than is immediately apparent in any given funeral and birth a greater purpose than is immediately apparent in the midst of labor. This conviction may be imperfectly expressed in the stories of Mithras slaying the bull, the inundations of the Nile, the primeval flood as punishment and promise, or even the Christ slain and raised; but no amount of contemporary rationalism or cynicism can erase this heartfelt conviction.

It is not just that life and death form an endless cycle. If ancient and contemporary holocaust and apocalypse have taught us anything, it is that life is not automatic. The possibility exists to exterminate life completely. No, for the cycle of life and death and new life to continue so doggedly, so persistently, so irrationally as to defy probability or perhaps even desirability, there must be some kind of chosen intervention.

• **The internal connection between divinity and humanity:** A greater intrinsic relationship binds human beings and divine spirit than is immediately apparent in the chronic trivialities of existence. We may not be players, but neither are we pawns. Some connection must link the moveable pieces on the chessboard and the cunning mind (or minds?) that shuffles us from one square to the next. Whether a divine spark is at war inside us with an original sin, or a Platonic demi-urge within us strives to break out, or a true humanity strives to be restored—something ties us to the divine that neither part can break. It is found in the three forms of love: *Eros, Agape, Phileos.*

It is not that a merely external relationship to the divine is unsatisfactory if one does not happen to be divine, but that it does not make ontological sense. It cannot make sense of the splashes of creativity that mark a Michelangelo or a Mahler, the bursts of genius that mark da Vinci or Einstein, the radical sacrifices that mark an Isaiah or a Mother Teresa, or the inexpressible joy that marks any ordinary woman or man in the experience of profound intimacy. Something noncoincidental—something in the very internal constitution of humanity—elevates us even for a moment beyond the cycle of birth and death.

• **The purposeful limitations of time and space:** A greater meaning waits to be discovered in, through, and beyond the limitations of existence than is immediately apparent in the hospital surgery or the coffee break on Monday afternoon. The movement from anticipation to fulfillment is generally experienced as a reduction in choices: *Because I am here and now, I cannot be anywhere else or at any other time.* We chafe and rage against such restrictions to our power and freedom. We rebel—that is, unless within the limitations of time and space some larger purpose does not so much reduce our choices as focus our priorities.

It is not that certain spaces or times are sacred or ordinary, but that all spaces and all times have the uneasy potential to be sacred or ordinary— and we do not always know which is which, or what it will be like tomorrow. This desert rock can suddenly become a ladder to heaven; this coffee room can become a temple; this surgery can become a gateway. These limitations, against which we rebel, are also the vehicles through which we discover meaning. The ancients knew: Without our freedom, we could not reach up; but without our bondage, God could not reach down.

• **The guarantee of ultimate hope:** A greater salvation beckons than the rulings of a judicial system or the vengeance of a vigilante. All the ancient religions find some way to redress the sufferings of victims, punish the victimizers, and allow for the finer distinctions that make it difficult to separate the one from the other. The contemporary legion of the lapsed, like those God-Fearers of the first century, began life with supreme confidence in the power of good education and enlightened politics. They believed in the achievability of the Pax Romana and the just society. No more. They look for a justice and a peace beyond the fragilities of institutions and the pride of men (specifically men, but also women).

It is not that the guarantee of salvation absolves humanity from moral life and spiritual discipline; but that it reassures us that the fact of "being human" will, after all, not be counted against us. Moreover, God-Fearers want the moral life and spiritual discipline to count for something…to somebody…at some time…in the end. The desire to lead a "worthy life" has not disappeared but, if anything, has grown stronger. The problem is that we are no longer clear on who God is, what that God might expect, and what a "worthy life" might look like.

Thus, the name "God-Fearer" is singularly appropriate. These legions of the lapsed (ancient and contemporary) are profoundly interested in spiritual things. Yet as the traditional religious institutions have collapsed, they have lost their bearings. In one sense, they are not panicking. They are sincere, intelligent, thoughtful, confident seekers who believe they still have time if they just keep looking. They are "godly" people. Yet in another sense, they are near despair. They have studied, conversed, experimented, searched, grieved, and are running out of time. In the end, they know there is hope, but they are not sure they are yet in the path of redemption. They are "godly" people—anxious, worried, stressed, uncertain, occasionally suicidal, and very afraid.

The ancient God-Fearer would not be as naïve as many popular spiritualists today in assuming that all "gods" were really the same "God" in disguise. No, many legitimate and logically contradictory views of the divine reign among the competing world religions. These competing views cannot all be reduced to a simple formula and a lowest common denominator of faith. What does exist are common threads, common themes of meaning, interwoven through all the religions of history—clues to a greater meaning that escapes any individual articulation. These modern God-Fearers are on a quest to put the clues together. They long for the infinite. They desire "God." And they really do mean to lead a "worthy life"—if only they can discern what it would look like.

ECHO'S JOURNAL _

I heard this same mentor speak in my philosophy class earlier this week and have been brooding on what he called "the ancient awe" ever since. Something exhilarates me when I realize that what is going on in my head also went on in the heads of the builders of the pyramids and the stone circles of Europe and preoccupied the minds of Socrates and Jesus and Mohammed.

"God-Fearers!" Yes, I think that is an apt description of my friends. We watch scary movies to avoid the biggest fright of all, glorying in our ability to be scared out of our wits and still eat popcorn. If we ever really met God, we would probably puke our guts out in anxiety. Perhaps the most frightening thing about God is that we don't know for sure exactly what should scare us the most.

It's interesting that we keep going back to fearful things: extreme sports, cocaine and ecstasy, high-speed entertainment, dangerous sex, dramatic career changes, and religion, of course. They're all risky things. They all involve crazy deeds and fearful falls. Something is attractive about God in a scary sort of way, as if by passing through the storm we might find a deeper peace, or a greater self-confidence, or a clarity of vision on the other side.

The mentor has invited his students back to the coffee shop for informal conversation—I think it is time I got to know what this person is all about.

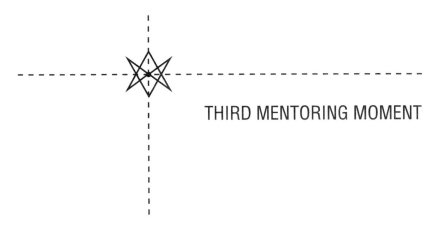

THIRD MENTORING MOMENT

The Once and Future Quest

Perhaps I exaggerate as I glorify the yearnings of the legion of the lapsed with the word *quest*. After all, degrees of earnestness stretch between relative contentment and restless passion. Most people with whom I speak (including professors, professionals, waitresses, and cab drivers) seem satisfied with the following classifications:

• **The spiritual dilettantes:** These people have strayed from their original religious roots to dabble in other religions, spiritualities, and undemanding philosophical generalizations. In the major life-cycle changes, they are still apt to return for the traditional wedding, infant baptism, bar mitzvah, and funeral; but they will continue to dabble in any religion to satisfy their limited curiosity and personal needs. They may already have set this book down and started to read something else.

• **The flaky fringe:** These people never had traditionally religious roots, or have forsaken those roots entirely. They investigate spiritualities that have no real historical grounding or cross-cultural significance. They will claim historic roots, but such claims are not particularly persuasive and have more to do with satisfying the government for charitable tax status than taking adherents deeper into faith. New age crystals, witches and warlocks, rites vaguely attributed to "druids," psychic communications with the dead, the sacrament of marijuana—all these may seem "flaky." Still, they represent a deeper and often earnest desire to quest for the infinite. They are angry that I have described them this way, but are so lively and diverse in their thinking that they will continue to read more and adapt it to their current passion.

• **The rationally reserved:** These people maintain real roots in the Enlightenment, in scientific methodology, and in the public education system of the nineteenth and twentieth centuries. Deeply reflective, ready to discuss, prepared to register for a seminar, their quest has been precipitated by quantum mechanics, process theologies, and a reassessment of classical and modern philosophy. They are professionals in any number of disciplines who are skeptical of "supernaturalism," but who warm to concepts of Truth, Beauty, Purpose, Order, and Meaning. They enjoy critical (likely very critical!) dialogue with this book, but will probably resist the practical ideas for daily spiritual discipline.

• **The seriously experimenting:** These pragmatic people will try anything once and work hard, provided they find the principles to be credible. They learn by doing, usually in a small group or pilgrim band, and will devote months and even years to a spiritual experiment before surrendering to the discipline or moving on to something else. They invest time, money, and energy to the practice of spirituality, but may not be the best people to explain coherently why they do it. They tend to think any generalization or abstraction to be but a slippery slope descending into "theology" and "doctrine," so they will probably enjoy the discipline in this book and shake their heads sadly over its conceptual foundation.

• **The radically committed:** These people merge theory and practice, theology and self-discipline, so completely that they willingly model an alternative lifestyle that shows contempt for the world and a mystical, even passionate, desire for God. These are the kind of people from whom the great monastic leaders of all faiths emerged. They manage to go to the extremes of individuality and community, freedom and obedience, prophecy and mendacity—all at the same time. They will appreciate the book, but will want to take its principles further, and deeper, and higher, than anyone can imagine.

Although most people seem to agree on the classifications of the lapsed, I find little agreement about who belongs in each classification. It is always easier to classify others than to classify oneself—and it is always wiser to work at classifying oneself than judging others. What is "flaky" to one might change, transform, and rescue another. What is "serious business" to one may seem a shallow, selfish, tempting sidetrack to another. If the individual members of the legion of the lapsed were completely honest with themselves (a rarity), they might well see themselves in all five classifications. This presentation is really intended for all five groups of people—although I sigh to think that in all probability the first two groups have already stopped listening.

This quest has a horizontal and a vertical dimension.

The horizontal dimension is the search to locate oneself in the cross-cultural population and multilayered environment of earth. Whether it's researching ancestry and antiques, appreciating macro- and micro-cultures from distant lands, or enjoying the neighborhood shopping center, the legion of the lapsed seek to understand their own lives by comparing them to equally viable life options. Whether it's advocating clean air, appreciating the many species of living (and dying) organisms that exist from one geological era to the next on this continent, or tending to an herb garden, the legion of the lapsed seek to discern their future by comparing humanity to life itself.

The horizontal dimension is a tension between fate and choice. Life, in all its cross-cultural and multienvironmental complexity, feels genetically sealed and socially determined. Careful examination of one's roots and life situation leads to the inexorable realization that *I am this…and I can be no other.* Yet even fate remains ambiguous. Advances in medical science and rapid changes in cultural norms are making the seemingly "inexorable" facts of life less certain. Handicaps can be overcome; genetic defects may be altered; traditional enemies may be reconciled; self-destructive habits may be changed. Even the limitations of gender might be burst—*if you choose it.* Yes, an element of life is existentially sealed and personally determined. A single choice, bold or timid, daring or haphazard, can change one's destiny forever. You face a *choice* about pregnancy, relationship, belonging, conviction, justice, wealth, health, and stealth that challenges fate for better or ill—*if you choose wisely.* No wonder the best-known prayer in the world among the legion of the lapsed is:

God grant me the serenity to accept the things I cannot change;
the courage to change the things I can;
and the wisdom to know the difference.

What began as a heartfelt prayer by alcoholics to free themselves from addiction became in the latter half of the twentieth century a gut-wrenching plea to an unknown god to be rescued from self-destructive behavior patterns forged by combinations of inexorable fate and persistently bad choices. And among these self-destructive behavior patterns from which the legion of the lapsed long to be rescued are the trappings of institutional religion itself.

The vertical dimension of this quest emerges inevitably from the horizontal human dilemma. Serenity, wisdom, and courage simply escape us. They are made possible only by the intersection of the infinite and the finite—the paradoxical and surprising appearance of the divine in the midst of the human condition. Without this vertical dimension, life becomes at best a "noble materialism." Life may have a philanthropic side, but even this is fundamentally motivated by self-interest. "Unless I share my abundance with the poor, they will eventually rise up anyway to take from me what they cannot get. Better to share now and stay safe, than withhold now and risk the security of my grandchildren." The only real difference between the noble materialism of those who "have" and the mere materialism of those who "have not" is enlightened selfishness combined with dumb luck. The ultimate expression of hope in the horizontal dimension is politics, and the ultimate expression of hopelessness is casino gambling. In a thoroughly materialistic society, it is no accident that the more cynical the public becomes about political elections and negotiations, the more casino gambling grows as a major industry and poker grows as the rising star of sports television.

This seemingly innate self-interest is the "stuff" of which the horizontal dimension is made. The religions of the East might call it pride, and the religions of the West might call it sin; but it is the matrix in which we are trapped. Courage is really just a form of ruthlessness; wisdom is just a form of cunning; and serenity is really just that fleeting moment when our needs have been sated by whatever "fix" is required at the time. We can dress it up. Affluence can make it more palatable. Education can make it more acceptable. Philanthropy can make it less of a burden on our conscience. However, bottom line, it is reality.

Or is it? Whatever their alienation from institutional religion might be, the legion of the lapsed feel equally alienated from this perception of reality. They are living Plato's famous metaphor of the cave. All this time their back has been to the fire, and their gaze has been fixed on the shadows playing on the wall. They had thought the shadows were real, until they began to wonder what had cast the shadows in the first place. They then turned to the fire, enjoyed its warmth and light for a time, but soon discovered that the fire of religious institutional life was limited and ultimately unsatisfying. But what if the fire itself is but another kind of imperfect projection? Douse the fire, and the shadows are *still there.* Could the warmth and light have another, greater, source? Could the cave have an opening—simultaneously an entrance for infinite light and warmth and an exit for finite limitation and yearning? Could a *reality* exist beyond the reality—a *new* being beyond the being?

- The fleeting contentment of our world might be an imperfect shadow of a greater serenity beyond it.
- The cunning of our world might be an imperfect shadow of greater purpose and universal wisdom.

• The ruthlessness that characterizes our world might be an imperfect shadow of a greater, purer courage.

In short, the illusion is the very self-interest that renders the world ultimately meaningless and powerless. Reality is something very different. The vertical dimension makes hope possible. Without it, only pathos or stoic fortitude remain—a common or a noble death, but death no less. With this vertical dimension we hope for more—a lasting meaning, a larger purpose, a vindicated life, and more.

Serenity Means "Life-at-Peace"

It is the synchronization of infinite meaning and daily living. It is not only the consciousness but also the unconsciousness (the intuition or the inner conviction) that personal identity has merged with infinite purpose. Serenity is an experience of perfect love for which sexual intercourse is only a faint shadow; it is an experience of unambiguous bliss for which contentment is but the merest hint. One can only speak of "life-at-peace" in metaphors, describe it in stories, convey it in images, and reenact it in rituals.

The ancients linked *Mythos* with serenity. Myth in its ancient expression was not a collection of superstitious stories and rigid rituals. Myth was a symbolic bridge between the finite and the infinite. Not only did it metaphorically point to important insights, but it opened the possibility of the divine communicating with the world. My mentor taught me that myth should not be evaluated as a means of transmitting *facts*, but as a means of communicating *truth*. Myth resists despair in a fleeting unity of reason and the depth of being.[1]

Wisdom Means "Life-in-Between"

It is the ability to make sense from ambiguity. Wisdom empowers the individual to act decisively and responsibly, whether or not the outcomes prove right or wrong. It is more than intelligence or reason. It is orderliness itself. Wisdom is the power to bring structure to chaos and logic to random thoughts. Wisdom is therefore a "word," an "act," a "creation" that separates land from water, history from survival, art from sense, and science from superstition. One can only experience "life-in-between" as a collage of action, reflection, invention, and meditation.

The ancients linked *Logos* with wisdom. Logos is the defining principle of reason itself, but also of nature, civilization, culture, and all forms that resist chaos. Logos is the reason there is "this" rather than "that." Logos is the force behind all logical continuity and historical predictability. It allows culture to be a vehicle for meaning, and it allows one to "make sense" of one's life, "set priorities" for one's actions, and "take responsibility" for one's successes or failures.

Courage Means "Life-on-the-Edge"

It is the motivation that lies behind radical self-affirmation and radical selflessness. Courage empowers the individual to risk everything for the sake of another, or for the sake of survival, or for the sake of the God. My mentor taught me that there are three kinds of courage:

- The courage to be a part, to surrender to relationship, and to merge with community, accepting limitations for the sake of the beloved;
- The courage to be oneself, to affirm one's individuality, and to dare to be unique, expanding one's identity beyond the expectations of others;
- The courage to accept acceptance, to be undeservedly blessed, to claim an ultimate concern, and to stake sanity itself on a deeper mystery.[2]

This is not the stoic courage of the purely horizontal dimension that desperately remains loyal to philosophical principles in a personal defiance of fate. It is a courage of the vertical dimension that affirms life and meaning in spite of threatening meaninglessness.

The ancients linked *Kairos* with courage. Kairos is time experienced as revelation rather than time experienced as chronology. It is not just a moment of insight, but a moment of being grasped by the infinite. Kairos is a moment when the infinite uses, shapes, and propels us for partially hidden purposes. The individual is held in the hands of God, swept away by the power of God, submerged in the import of God. Kairos elicits courage; courage stands unbending before the onslaught of Kairos. The three kinds of courage are really not possible outside of a sense of "the momentous." A moment, a time, becomes pregnant with meaning and explodes with significance, requiring courage both to endure it and to follow its implications to the very end.[3]

The movement from *Mythos* to *Logos* to *Kairos* helps explain the classifications within the legion of the lapsed I mentioned earlier. The "spiritual dilettantes" and the "flaky fringe" tend to be preoccupied by myth and strive for "life-at-peace." They cannot achieve it, however, until they go deeper into the Logos of meaning. The "rationally reserved" and the "seriously experimenting" explore "life-in-between" to create, innovate, and think, but cannot overcome the ambiguities of life. The "radically committed" take increasing risks, courageously limiting themselves in relationships, expanding their selfhood beyond public expectations, and surrendering to the infinite.

God grant me the serenity to accept the things I cannot change;
the courage to change the things I can;
and the wisdom to know the difference.

Alcoholics may have been the first to use this prayer widely, but it has now been claimed by anyone seeking freedom from the entrapment of self-destructive patterns (personal and universal) through the intervention of a Higher Power.

ECHO'S JOURNAL _

Yes, I think I am among the "seriously experimenting," and I am surprised to see how many of us there are. What you are is a matter of perspective, of course. No doubt my grandparent Boomers would prefer me to be among the "spiritual dilettantes," flitting from spirituality to spirituality but never risking getting too close to the light. Their parents would have regarded me as on the "flaky fringe." My boss would prefer me to be "rationally reserved," sensing that a little spiritual enthusiasm is good for staff morale, but too much might scare away the clients.

I am what I am—but I will be whatever I choose to be. That paradox is the source of my neurosis. I have always considered paradoxical inconsistency an accident of culture, but now I am wondering if it is an eternal predicament. Or perhaps the result of a primordial nervous breakdown that pre-dates (and exacerbates) my personal anxieties.

I am familiar with the "serenity prayer," of course. Who isn't, these days? I've got friends who recite the mantra who aren't even abusing any substances! It's the "serenity" part that escapes us. Occasionally, I can accept the things I cannot change (especially if I don't really want to change them in the first place); and occasionally, I can change the things I can (especially if the change is not too difficult or expensive). I can find the wisdom to sort those things out, but I can't seem to find the wisdom to know when to refuse to accept the unacceptable and when to surrender to unacceptable acceptance. Fate is a funny thing. I can find my way inside the box and can even take tentative steps out of the box, but if I really push the edges to go beyond the box of fate entirely, I am utterly at a loss.

I begin to see that at any given moment, on any given day, my life may be "edgy" or "between"…and occasionally "peaceful." What is more illuminating is that the cause of being one or the other may have as much to do with Spirit as it does with the roller coaster that is my life.

What makes me "edgy" has to do with newness—new idea, new relationship, new career, new something. What if "newness" itself was not just haphazard, but occurred with a hidden intentionality? What if it was, for better or worse, "meant to be"? Kairos? Me?

I think hardest when I am hardest pressed. I suspect it is not as advanced as logic. It is more like mere cunning, and it has a lot to do with just surviving to the next day; but it is thought no less. Figure it out! Find a way! Think! If there were no deeper order and predictability—no hope of manipulation and control, no structure at all—I think I would just give up and die. Even the worst cynics I know, those who claim to believe in nothing at all, are remarkably certain that the sun will rise in the morning and set at night. "One day at a time," says Alcoholics Anonymous. There is wisdom in that. It keeps you from suicide.

The link between peace and myth escapes me at the moment. I see it from afar, but do not yet grasp it. I always considered myth to be another word for "falsehood," and suddenly it is the methodology of meaning. (Those are the mentor's words, not mine. Too sophisticated for me. Beyond my grasp. Yet they imply something I need to understand).

I begin to understand my greatest, deepest real fear. I am afraid that when push comes to shove and life reduces itself to a razor's edge of decision or fate, I will be revealed to be a coward. I'm not sure that I have the guts for a real relationship or the audacity for total self-expression or the courage for anyone or anything to hold me when I am at my most despicable and dirty. I fear I will run away again and hide. I talk with the mentor again tomorrow, and I fear what he will see.

FOURTH MENTORING MOMENT

Discerning Your Position in Life with Infinite Perspective

The individual must understand: *The infinite is not neutral to your total personal growth.* The infinite's lack of neutrality to the finite may be kind, but it may also be unkind. It may be caring, and it may be hostile. It may be a comforting ocean, or a devouring fire. The finite's "desire for God" is matched, even overmatched, by the infinite's desire for your total personal growth.

The Eros of your life is only a spark of the greater Eros that burns in the heart of God. Eros is the passion, the desire for self-expression, creativity, and unity with the fullness of meaning. It is the desire to understand, even as we have been fully understood; "to know" in the sense of "to merge." Eros on the part of the finite is not a desire for explanations, but for purpose. Eros on the part of the infinite is not a desire to absorb, but to fulfill.

The weakness in Plato's metaphor of the cave is that the story itself offers no real reason or incentive why any person should turn away from the shadows to look first to the fire and then further to the light outside. Plato himself admitted that this "turning around" could not be mere coincidence. It was an "urge," a sudden compulsion, or an instinct— and this instinct itself is the infinite acting upon the finite. It is no random accident that the finite reaches up and out to the infinite, but some spark of the divine within us that instinctively seeks to reunite with the fire or with the greater illumination of God. Plato's disciples elaborated a great chain of being in which various "demi-urges" passed human consciousness on and on, up the ladder, until the human soul finally merged with infinite being; but the mystical core of ancient thought requires no such mediation. The soul flies to God and God flies to the finite soul, as lovers fly to each other's arms.

Such desire forces the finite and the infinite to intersect. Human experience is a kind of "mirrored Eros" in which the human reaches up, straining to touch the infinite, yearning to unite with the divine; and the divine reaches down, shattering human constructions and rationalizations of God and reshaping the patterns of meaning that give life purpose and hope.

Humanity Reaches Up

The human reaches up and out. Out of the soulful depths of human experience the human reach rises above the plane of one's immediate world. What elevates human yearning above the plane of mere existence is the recognition that *life is a struggle, not something simply to be endured,* and the recognition that there are *relationships of mentoring that help us grow, not just cooperatives that help us survive.* The finite is a flow of experience in which intimate beginnings, life struggles, and spiritual coaching are the key moments in the pursuit of purposefulness.

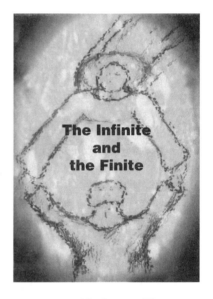

The Infinite and the Finite

- *Intimate Beginnings* are experiences pregnant with change. They may be psychological and therapeutic, educational and philosophical, relational and sexual, criminal or philanthropic. They are so intimate that they usually escape public attention, yet decisively change the course of a life. And it is not always clear whether the change is for the better or worse.

- *Life Struggle* is the experience of living with consequences, either as victor or victim. Life struggle is demographic change lived out in the individual defined by age, marital status and family, income and ownership, culture and ethnicity, education, occupation, location, mobility, taste and lifestyle, and religion. Life struggle encompasses all the triumphs and tragedies lived in that demographic matrix. Life struggle is the experience of time as *Chronos,* the moment-to-moment passage of time that leads inexorably to death.

• *Spiritual Coaching* is the experience of mentors and guides along the way. They may be long- or short-term relationships and vary in degree or scope of profundity. Their coaching may contain good and/or bad advice, but their influence is extraordinary. They help interpret infinite beginnings and cope with life struggles in ways that can lead either to glory or to disgrace.

These key elements define our desire to escape the entrapment of finitude, exit the "cave" of our existence, and merge with God. My mentor summarized the critique of existentialism by saying that the infinite empowers humanity to confront the three great anxieties of life:[1]

1. *The anxiety of fate and death*: The unsettling fear that grips you in every tragic funeral and personal loss and that compels you to take drugs, experiment with diet plans, exercise until you faint, and prolong your life as long as possible.

2. *The anxiety of emptiness and meaninglessness*: The unsettling fear that grips you in every broken relationship, every career change, and every relocation—or that shakes your confidence with every gratuitous experience of evil and every brutal terrorist attack.

3. *The anxiety of guilt and condemnation*: The unsettling fear that grips you with every moral failure, every little act of irresponsibility, and every image of a hungry child or yet another victim of AIDS, or every polluted stream.

The key elements of intimate beginnings, life struggle, and spiritual coaching tip the balance between despair and hope. They only become possible when the infinite penetrates the finite. These three elements, therefore, represent the essential points of connection through which the finite can communicate with the infinite.

Humans fundamentally communicate with the infinite as we experience intimate beginnings, life struggle, and spiritual coaching. Traditional developmental psychology teaches us that we are most vulnerable to change our lifestyle and our attitudes at certain stages of the life cycle, such as at the birth of a baby, coming of age as an adult, marriage or divorce, and death. Indeed, institutional religion has come to mark these life cycle stages with ritual. The truth, however, is that this vulnerability to the infinite does not come in "stages" at all, but in a constant and unpredictable barrage of everyday experience.

- This connection with the infinite happens whenever we experience some new form of intimacy, be it a harmless flirtation, a new friendship, or deep love. It happens whenever we experience a new bond, whether it be with a new community, a dynamic process, or a great mission.

- It happens whenever we struggle *against* despair, when we fight for a cause or simple survival. It happens whenever we stand up to intimidation, break control, strive for justice, or battle with our addictions.

- It happens whenever we give or receive sincere and urgent mentoring, whether it is a matter of simple advice, career counseling, or guidance from the confessional. It happens whenever we give or receive any communication of significance beyond conversations about such mundane topics as the weather or sports scores.

At any time of the day or week, these moments emerge when we are vulnerable to the infinite and when we can communicate with the infinite. The infinite invades our existence for radical change, clearer purpose, and deeper meaning.

Divinity Reaches Down

The divine reaches down. Out of the sublime heights of infinite experience the divine reach penetrates beneath the plane of the present moment. Divine penetration reveals that life can be different. We can be liberated from the self-destruction that entraps us. The mundane and the inevitable can be imbued with deeper purpose. They do not have to lead to hopeless despair. Forms of thought and cultural constructions can be vehicles to meaning, not just arbitrary, self-centered whims. The infinite is a flow of experience in which infinite beginnings, reasonable order, and patterns of meaning are the key elements in the fulfillment of greater purpose.

- *Kairos* (infinite beginnings) are moments of revelation and apocalyptic change. The world is turned upside down and inside out. The totally unexpected happens, and the completely impossible occurs. Life and one's perspective on life will never be the same again. And at the apocalyptic moment, we are not always clear whether the change is for the better or worse.

- *Logos* (reasonable order) produces predictable patterns of mind and nature. These rational interpretations, scientific deductions, and intellectual habits make sense of the world and our lifestyles. Such patterns are the platform for discovery and innovation as well as the foundation for our everyday interaction with the world around us.

• *Mythos* (meaning patterns) includes constellations of symbols, stories, and purposeful activities through which decision making is justified and lives have purpose. Constellations of meaning are approximations of truth. Their pragmatic purpose is to form community, encourage peaceful interaction, encourage productivity, provide comfort, and reveal the future.

These are the enduring characteristics of the infinite that invade the moments of our existence at our times of greatest vulnerability or openness. We may be conscious or unconscious of their impact to shape and direct our lives, yet the more we focus our attention on them, the more God and Soul merge—the stronger we become to resist despair, risk action, and seek guidance.

Key Empowerments

The experience of the infinite empowers us to confront the fundamental anxieties of life. The infinite rescues us from cynicism, selfishness, despair—and suicide. The infinite produces possibilities, creative potentials, and hope.

1. *Kairos* empowers us to confront the anxiety of fate and death. The apocalyptic power of God liberates us from entrapment by the past or the present and opens the possibility for new birth and a fresh start. Kairos represents the hope that life is not as inevitable or remorseless as it seems. A Higher Power with a vested interest in existence can and will interrupt logic and reshape meaning.

2. *Logos* empowers us to confront the anxiety of emptiness and meaninglessness: God's reasonable order brings order from chaos and provides the foundation for strategic planning and realizable goals. The predictability and reliability of the structure of existence allows us to understand why life is as it is and helps us prepare for life as it will be. Human reason is possible because it connects with a large, even more complex, order in the universe.

3. *Mythos* empowers us to confront the anxiety of guilt and condemnation. God's purposefulness offers forgiveness and acceptance, and a method for harmonizing our behavior with an infinite destiny. Mythos allows us to bring meaning to existence, interpreting the significance of events for our relationships, identities, and purposes.

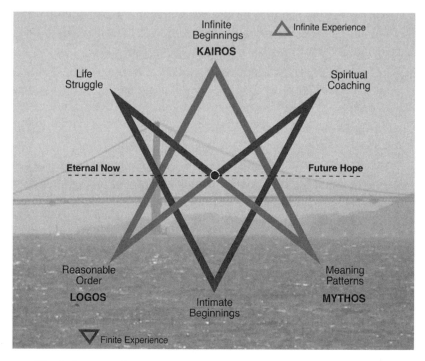

The influence of Kairos, Logos, and Mythos make intimate beginnings, life struggle, and spiritual coaching possible and productive. In a sense, these are already embedded in the soul of humanity. Together they are the intuition, motivation, or Platonic "urge" that turns human consciousness from shadows to light, drawing the soul to God.

The diagram above images the intersection of the infinite experience and finite reality. The image is important, because the intersection of infinite and finite can be cast against any snapshot of daily living. Any time an image touches or moves us, this internal dynamic is revealed. Further reflection lets us discern both our current situation and our options for the future. Our current situation reveals our particular vulnerability to the infinite at any given time.

Chronos as the mere passage of time differs from *existence* as the lived experience of time passing. On the one side of this intersection of infinite and intimate beginnings lies only struggle and inevitability, but on the other side of this intersection lies the possibility of spiritual guidance and patterns of meaning. Existence has significance. Humans are self-consciously aware of their existence, and this alone suggests an intrinsic value and purposefulness to living.

The plane of intersection (marked by the horizontal dotted line) is the timeline of our existence. The ancients would have understood it to be Chronos—the inexorable passage of minutes, hours, and years leading to our inevitable death. The depth of being (hidden beneath our everyday existence) is made up of three realities perceived as being within the control or influence of the individual.

- *Reasonable Order.* This is the experience of structure, predictability, and reasonable interpretation of life experience. We are convinced that the scientific or rational investigation of existence will lend meaning and purpose to our inevitable death and that to a degree we can control or influence that purpose.

- *Intimate Beginnings*: These are the choices for relationships— friendships, animosities, sexual encounters, marriages, networks, and associations—with which we sort the passage of time into experiences of healing or hope. We are convinced that the ability to shape peace, harmony, health, or intimacy will lend meaning and purpose to our inevitable death and will provide something of worth that will outlast our time span.

- *Meaning Patterns*: These are the philosophies, lifestyles, artistic expressions, and religious perspectives with which we measure success and evaluate our lives. We are convinced that human imagination or speculative conceptualization can explain evil and predict the course of history.

Much of our time on earth is devoted to exploring this depth of being. Yet an equal share of our time on earth is devoted to exploring the power of being (hidden beyond our everyday existence). The power or "potential" of being is made up of three realities that are perceived as being beyond the control or influence of the individual.

- *Life Struggle*: Fate may be experienced as intrusions upon the ordered predictability of life. Disease, divorce, bankruptcy, war, natural disaster, and any number of other unwanted and unanticipated events will throw our existence into turmoil.

- *Infinite Beginnings*: Fate may be experienced as miraculous luck or unexpected hope that turns life around and lifestyles inside out.

- *Spiritual Coaching.* Fate may be experienced as unexpected insight or illumination precipitated by some unlikely encounter with another human being.

The passage of time that is our existence is not the blind pursuit of survival akin to the experience of all other organisms and species on earth. "Being human" means that we inevitably look beneath and beyond the plane of our existence, and this may be for either selfish or altruistic motives. We look to the depth of being and the power of being because there simply *must be more* than mere survival. The very *consciousness* that there must be more is the verification that somehow, somewhere, there *is more* than survival.

In the diagram above, the various dots on the plane of our existence represent our spiritual position at any given time. Sometimes I may be deeply suffering, caught in the paradox between irrational evil and the conviction that there must be an explanation of all things. At other times, I may be swept away by changes to my emotions or my lifestyle, caught in the paradox between desire and obligation. Or at still other times, I may be searching for meaning, caught in the paradox between skepticism toward formerly sacred assumptions and the longing for spiritual guidance.

The plane of existence tests humanity with three attitudes of courage. Each attitude confronts one of the fundamental existential anxieties. Each attitude becomes possible because of the intersection of the depth of being and the power of being.

1. The courage to separate confronts the existential anxiety of fate and death, and empowers us to live "life-on-the-edge." This is the courage of individualization, independence, self-definition, and self-expression commonly associated with *eros*. It is the courage to change.

2. The courage to participate confronts the existential anxiety of meaninglessness and emptiness, and empowers us to live "life-in-between." This is the courage of cooperation, unity, self-compromise, and relationship commonly associated with *phileos*. It is the essence of wisdom.

3. The courage to accept acceptance confronts the existential anxiety of guilt and condemnation, and empower us to live "life-at-peace." This is the courage of unity, forgiveness, self-surrender, and calm commonly associated with *agape*. It is the hope of serenity.

The religious background you bring to the experience of the intersection of the infinite and the finite will influence your meditation on the talisman. You have a unique way to ponder every snapshot of daily living that touches your soul, stirs your memory, or moves you to deeper emotion. My own background, for example, is clearly Christian (both Roman Catholic and Lutheran from the Eastern European side of my family, and Protestant and Methodist from the American side of my family). That Christian background is brought to any significant snapshot of my life and influences how I use the talisman to interpret my life situation in infinite perspective.

ECHO'S JOURNAL –

The finite reaches up even as the infinite reaches down. I am not sure that it is quite fair to personalize that statement. It does not seem quite comprehensive enough to say that "I" reach up even as "God" reaches down. Yet surely that is a part of what is happening, at least.

No doubt my spirit reaches up—right, left, up, down—out of myself, out into something more, out toward some truth, reality, or hope that escapes my imagination, articulation, and control. I tell myself sometimes that I am a fool, that there is "nothing there." Yet the very fact that calling myself a fool "makes sense" suggests that some larger truth exists before which my life can be evaluated, assessed, or judged. And if "something" can declare me "fool," then perhaps something can vindicate me as "wise," and therefore, something must be "out there" to reach for. It may escape my grasp, but it always motivates my reach. Why bother with art, science, relationship—or even eating, sleeping, and talking—if it were otherwise?

I had always thought that any confidence that this "infinite" might be reaching down toward me was simply a "leap of faith." Now I am beginning to think it a reasonable anticipation.

It is the experience of intimacy that has always paved the way to the infinite for me. It is the difference between friendship and acquaintance, birth and replication, or sex and pornography. The latter is always so selfish. It leads inevitably and drearily back to oneself. The former is always so selfless. It leads inevitably and ecstatically beyond oneself. There is someone— something—"wholly other" than me. It is beautiful. It is good. It is more real and timeless than any other human activity. It's as if I see God in every act of love-making, or love-receiving, or both/and.

There really is a depth to being—a penetration of the infinite into the finite that goes to the heart of reality. Intimacy, reasonableness, meaning— I see this now. Beyond any particular expression or example, activity, or religion, a common experience of these things lives among all creatures. But such depth would be hopeless if there were not also a power to being— ecstasy, struggle, guiding leadership—continually renewing the intimacy, redefining the reasonableness, and reshaping the meaning. I begin to see that now.

I have begun to explore the "map" the mentor gave us. It is unlike any other "map" I have ever used. It doesn't tell me what to do. It tells me how to be. I'm not even sure what that means! Today, for example, was a bad day: constant struggle, overwhelming trivialities, serious hurt, constant frustration, a combined onslaught of the stupidity of people and the indifference of life. Using the map, I began to look for patterns of meaning, lessons for survival, higher visions of what might sustain me. I became aware of my capacity to think on the one hand and the value of the advice from my best friends on the other hand. I found myself moving away from frantic struggle to a separate peace. It was a serenity of sorts, an inkling of greater possibilities.

Yet I am not at all confident that hope is real. The infinite is an abstraction to me. God is a stranger, simultaneously too big to be embraced and too small to deserve to be embraced. It's an infinite parallel to my finite predicament. I am not altogether confident that I am real. The finite is an abstraction to me. I am a stranger to myself, simultaneously too important to be ignored and too small to be preserved. Tomorrow the mentor is addressing a gathering of Christian clergy; perhaps he may offer some resolution to this impossible situation.

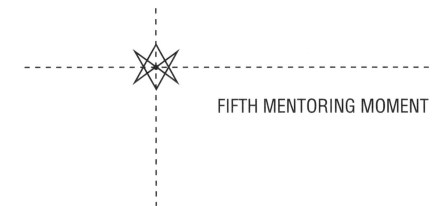

The Experience of Christ

When the infinite and the finite intersect in the plane of our existence, the intersection ceases to be abstract. Intersection becomes incarnation. It is a real, tangible, sensory presence—yet cannot be contained in any real, tangible, sensory way. It can be experienced, but not encompassed. It can be studied, but not fully understood. Incarnation is not rationalization. The individual does not so much come to know the object of his or her attention as to become known by the object of his or her attention. One does not draw Jesus the Christ to himself, but one is drawn into Jesus the Christ.

The ancient Chalcedonian Confession succinctly summarizes the incarnation as this intersection of the infinite and the finite. Jesus is the Christ because he reveals most fully and clearly this paradoxical merging of divine and human spirit.

> *Jesus, fully human and fully divine, infinite paradox, crucial for abundant life.*

Since the Enlightenment and the emergence of scientific methodology, scholars have conducted successive "quests for the historical Jesus." These quests have become increasingly pedantic and irrelevant. They seek to *prove or debunk* belief in the divinity of Christ by demonstrating if he actually lived and what he actually said. Of course, this is asking too much of archeological and exegetical science. The various quests simply lead to quarrels of interpretation, which may gain some scholars tenure at a university, but which have little impact on the *existence* of real people. No one is interested in the *chronology* of Jesus (or the sayings of Pharaoh

Akhenaton, for that matter) and how that relates to the *chronology* of our lives. We may be distinctly interested in the *existence* of Jesus and how that impacts the *existence* of our lives.

"Existence" is more than "chronology," even though scientific theory since the beginning of the Enlightenment has sought to reduce it to that. We only become aware of "existence" at all when we see the shadows on the wall (in Plato's metaphor) and intuit an infinite reality beyond our small campfire. "Existence" is made possible by the intersection of the infinite and the finite. Without that intersection, we are left with "chronology." "Existence" is the intuition of *something more...from which we remain distant or alienated.* It is the struggle to find, return, or reunite to that "something more" to which Jesus becomes supremely relevant.

The only possible value to any "quest for the historical Jesus" lies in this deeper quest to *reunite with the divine.* Why else should we be interested? Only when we have experienced this intersection of the infinite and the finite—caught a glimmering of it from the corner of our eyes, or felt the presence of it at the center of our lives, or seen the joy of it in the behavior of the "saints"—is our curiosity and passion aroused to explore the nuances of the life of Jesus. The life of Jesus becomes a clue, symbol, or talisman through which we might commune with God.

The identity of Jesus articulated in the ancient Christianity of the Chalcedonian Confession as this paradigmatic intersection of the infinite and the finite indicates his significance for the possibilities of courage (life-on-the-edge), wisdom (life-in-between), and serenity (life-at-peace). Whatever our current life situation, we are vulnerable to Christ in six distinct ways. In other words, our human need intersects with God's grace in different ways, at different moments in our lives.[1] I have come to see how these six perspectives on Jesus the Christ actually serve as points of contact with our existential needs and spiritual yearnings and can become a focus for meditation—*a device for the global positioning of the soul.*

The incarnation of the infinite (which I describe here as "Jesus the Christ") is experienced in six primary ways—corresponding to the primary experiences and yearnings of life. I have used the more human and ordinary name *Jesus* to describe those three experiences that originate from the depth of being: the Promise Keeper, the Healer, and the Spiritual Guide. I have used the more cosmic and extraordinary name *Christ* to describe those three experiences that originate from the power of being: the New Being, the Perfect Human, and the Vindicator. These aspects of Jesus the Christ intersect as an infinite paradox on the plane of our existence.

Therefore, the diagram also guides the meditative mind to discern *where this point of contact with Jesus the Christ will lead.* It suggests the import or direction that will draw the individual deeper into the spiritual life.

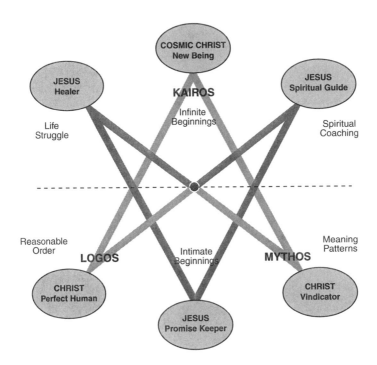

Jesus the Christ is an *experience* of the intersection of the infinite and the finite and cannot be limited to any one expression of that paradox. Christianity has many definitions of saving grace. In the New Testament alone at least five alternative views explain how people may be "saved"! None of them grasps the fullness and mystery of how the intersection of the infinite with the finite, represented in the incarnation, is the hope of existence. It is the mystical experience itself—beyond words, or dogmas, or doctrines, or liturgies, or sacraments, of the God above gods in the depths of existence—that is the real nature of salvation. We just experience it, interpret it, and articulate it in various ways.

Experiencing the Cosmic Christ, the New Being

The Cosmic Christ is beyond imagination and definition and, therefore, beyond invocation and control. He is the "Unexpected One." He is the Devouring Fire, the Earth Shaker, the Tsunami of Grace, and the Whirlwind. He is the Thief in the Night and the Unknown God. He is the Life Changer, the Shatterer and the Builder, the Architect of Existence, and the Star Shepherd. Ultimately, the Cosmic Christ is the Word of Life, the living message that connects to our finite existence and creates new being out of old, unexpected life in the face of death.

In the midst of mystery and threat of infinite beginnings, the Cosmic Christ, the New Being, stretches out to connect with our need. It is the power of being reaching into the depths of being. My mentor used the term *New Being* to express the radical nature of this intervention.[2] These are the moments of awe and terror, a Kairos in which something radically new and of profound import is shaking one's life—but what it means and how life will change remain unclear. The Kairos penetrates the Chronos of our daily life deep into the roots of our lives, simultaneously confirming and shattering our rational order, simultaneously shattering and creating our interpretations of God and World.

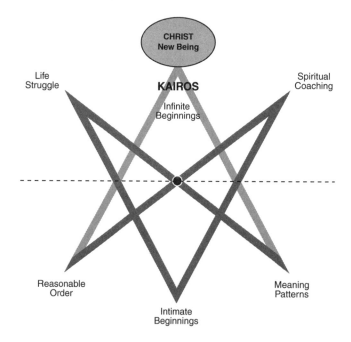

The New Being is experienced both "prophetically" and "apocalyptically." The prophetic challenges our reason, our sense of the predictable and the appropriate. The apocalyptic challenges our mythologies, our sense of balance and harmony. The word *apocalyptic* is *not* the same as *apocalypse.* Apocalyptic experience is about turning one's life upside down and inside out—radically transforming and redirecting one's lifestyle. It is not about a "judgment day," but there may well be a sense of judgment about one's past that beckons repentance. It is not about destruction and chaos, but there may well be a sense of old habits ruined and life in disorder. Apocalyptic experience, however, is fundamentally hopeful. It brings an implicit promise of something better, something more valuable, toward which radical change is leading.

Therefore, the "next steps" after experiencing the New Being include the development of meaning patterns to interpret the experience, and the reconstruction of one's lifestyle to restore predictability and "reasonable order." Kairos is always momentary, and one cannot remain there for long without jeopardizing sanity or survival. Yet there are times in life when such apocalyptic experience is necessary to shatter rituals that are no longer meaningful and to destroy structures that have become too limiting. Remember that apocalyptic experience always implies a degree of ethical ambiguity. The reestablishment of ethical norms is part of the new quest for meaning patterns and reasonable order.

New Being Right Now

Bill J. is a successful senior executive for a major corporation. Yet in a single year he experiences the breakup of his marriage, alienation from his children, the loss of his home, and intense dissatisfaction with his career—and he experiences an unsettling intimacy with another woman, a reconnection with his university student daughter, the acquisition of a downtown apartment, and an opportunity to become CEO of a nonprofit organization at a greatly reduced salary. In such a Kairos experience Bill does not know whether to be terrified or exhilarated, guilty or liberated, depressed or optimistic. His life is being demolished and reconstructed, and he is only partly in control of the process. To survive and, indeed, thrive, he must develop a "mythology" or pattern of meaning with which to interpret his loss and growth. He must also establish new structures of behavior that redefine his identity in accord with former and future relationships.

The Cosmic Christ has unexpectedly changed and shaped Bill's life. Bill does not know whether to weep or rejoice, rage in anger or give thanks. Both and neither seem appropriate. He has been swept away. His doctor is worried about his blood pressure and the danger of a stroke or heart attack. Much of what he intuited was wrong with his life has been altered, and yet much of what he valued in life has been sacrificed to do it. Bill's first reaction was to feel guilt. He still feels guilty. Yet he has gone beyond guilt. He is shocked, astonished, surprised. If life has come apart, it also seems that life is coming together—not perfectly, not unambiguously, but differently. Maybe there is hope for him yet. He needs to experience the Cosmic Christ.

Experiencing Christ the Perfect Human

The Perfect Human is usually approached as an approximation, a metaphor, and fiction of literature or as a projection of imagination. Yet Jesus is *real.* He is flesh and blood, yet perfect. He is the Eternal Friend, the Addiction Free, the Sinless, the Clearly Good Person. He is the New Adam, God's Own Child. He is the Sacrificial Lamb without Blemish, the example of Ultimate Generosity. Christ the Perfect Human is the Word Made Flesh, the archetype of suffering, endurance, and victory.

In the midst of the structures of reason, inflexible logic, and the seeming inevitability of cause and effect, Christ, the Perfect Human, stretches out to find the credible mentors who can distill truth from knowledge and free the spirit from bondage to self-destructive behavior. It is the power of being at work in the depths of being.

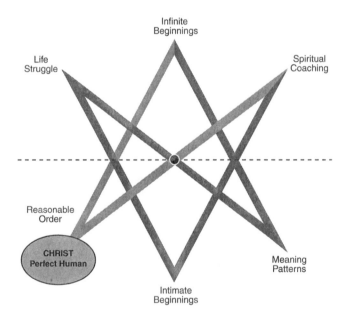

Jesus the Christ is described in ancient Christian writing as the "True Man" or the "New Adam." He embodies what humanity was originally created to be prior to the "fall" into the real world of cause and effect and inevitable death. He is truly, fully, perfectly "human"—without the "original sin" that sabotages the best efforts and most sincere wishes of humanity. The perfect human is an ethical paradigm for all humanity, but even more than this the perfect human is the original prototype of what God destines humanity to become. Here is the one, true child of God, through whom we can be adopted as fellow heirs of the original garden of Eden: perfect in wisdom, perfect in relationships, perfect in righteousness, perfect in health, perfect in wisdom.

"Original sin" in contemporary terminology is best translated as "addiction." Addiction is the number one health issue in the world today. An addiction is any self-destructive behavior pattern that we chronically deny—and yet that inevitably robs life of meaning and inevitably brings death. More people are trapped by self-destructive behavior patterns such as this than at any other time in history. Addiction is a much broader affliction than mere substance abuse. Any habit of mind and body can become a self-destructive pattern of behavior. Its ultimate source is classically understood as "pride"—absolute self-centeredness, the elevation of self to ultimate concern. The public longs to know a truly addiction-free human being—a perfect human being—who is entirely free of self-interest.

The language of addiction intervention helps us understand the function of the Perfect Human in the depths of being. The addict must first "bottom out"—confront despair, face the inevitability of death—before becoming able to experience the intervention of the "Higher Power." This radical intervention of the New Being must connect with the mentoring of wise spiritual coaches who can combine radical honesty with deep compassion. Such mentors help people experience the intervention of a Higher Power that can liberate us from the inevitability of our habits, allowing a "new person" or a "new creation" to emerge from the old life. What was not possible to accomplish, despite every effort of therapy and education, becomes possible because the infinite can break the rules that govern the finite.

Perfectly Human Right Now

Wally S. is an engineer with a large corporation. He has a Ph.D. from M.I.T., an enormous income, a beautiful home, a loving family. He has never read classic literature, has no particular appreciation for fine art, and never studied a language in college other than DOS. His favorite music is Bach because the music is so mathematical, and the only place he can hear Bach is in his local church, which is why he belongs. Wally is a brilliant worker. He is also obsessed with his career, sports cars, and proving his manhood with women. An occasional user of the drug ecstasy, he has become a boastful alcoholic. He has been in therapy for several years and has tried to commit suicide at least twice (in the certain knowledge of his third wife). He is one of the rapidly growing demographic of highly intelligent, wealthy, desperate people in America.

Alcoholics Anonymous might be the breakthrough Wally needs, but he remains convinced that his situation is the inevitable result of his DNA, social upbringing, and education. He stubbornly believes that his course is largely determined by his own judgment (which he vehemently swears is not impaired in any way). Yet already he is searching for a mentor, some person who might connect him with infinite power to restore his innocence, health, and freedom. His wife thinks, "If only his church would stop fighting over organ music and the Nicene Creed and introduce him to the addiction-free Jesus, he might have a chance."

Wally needs a friend, but not just any friend. Indeed, part of his irascibility is that no relationship really suffices. He searches for a perfect relationship. He looks for a role model without judgment. He yearns for a friend who will never let him drive carelessly, who will always tell him the truth even when he rails against it, and who can empathically take upon himself the pains of withdrawal. Wally's greatest problem is that he feels this friend can only, inevitably, be a figment of imagination and a literary invention. His skepticism knows no boundary, because every promising relationship has proven to be, at best, a limited approximation. Wally does not believe this friend exists. Eventually, he may kill himself because of it. He needs to experience Christ the Perfect Human.

Experiencing Christ the Vindicator

An orderly, predictable universe is meaningless unless it includes a righteous, inevitable, morality. Christ is the Vindicator, the personification of justice. He is the Righteous Judge the King of Kings, and the Protector of the Innocent. He is the Dragon Slayer, the Harrower of Hell, and the Liberator. He is the Sword of Truth, the Revealer, and the Light Bringer…the Defender of the Poor, the Rescuer of the Oppressed, the Evaluator of Souls, and the Advocate for the Abused. He is King of Kings, President of Presidents, Chief Justice of all courts, and Prince of Peace. If the Cosmic Christ is the Word of Life, and Christ the Perfect Human is the Word Made Flesh, then Christ the Vindicator is the Last Word.

In the midst of all the competing religions of the world—and all the competing mythologies of nationalism, science, and business, which have rituals, slogans, creeds, and tribunals like the religions of the world—Christ the Vindicator stretches out to connect our individual life struggles

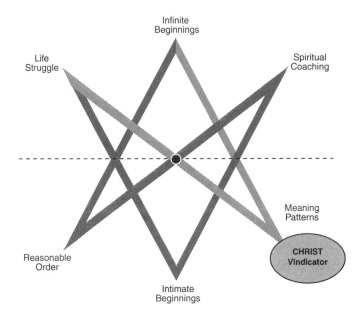

with that spark of eternal significance that seems to dance just beyond our peripheral vision.

Vindication is a deeper experience of justice, in which individuals are cherished for their ultimate worth in the eyes of their accusers, in the self-perceptions of their own souls, and in the sight of God. This is not merely a class struggle or an economic struggle. It is a struggle against the powers of victimization themselves. The real pain of life struggle is not that we are hurt, but that we are demeaned. Victimization is an experience of undeserved evil, disproportionate pain, and the theft of our self-esteem. Hurt a person, and you take away the person's rights; abuse a person, and you take away hope. Rights can be restored by legal action, but hope can only be restored by a deeper vindication that reconnects life with infinite significance.

Vindication is really not about liberation, but about recovery and surrender to patterns of meaning that cleanse a person of shame, equip a person with empowering interpretations of life, and articulate a good reason to hope for tomorrow. Jesus is a paradigm of the vindicator. Numerous stories of his life concern the vindication of one who was victimized. He rescues the adulteress threatened by stoning, touches lepers with healing and encouragement, and spends time with sinners, Samaritans, and outcasts. His goal is not to put them in touch with a legal system to defend their rights, nor even to plead their case to governments to change public policies. Jesus introduces them to an alternative pattern of meaning and significance that will give them hope.

Vindication Now

Antonia is a lawyer in the criminal justice system. She has been a state prosecutor and is now a private defense lawyer. Operating on both sides of the courtroom, she has learned one thing: It is not as easy to distinguish the rights of the accused, the rights of the accusers, and the rights of the victims as television would have us believe. In fact, the ambiguities are only increasing exponentially because in the emerging world victimization has become a way of life. It is scripted into daily living. Today's victim becomes tomorrow's abuser; yesterday's criminal becomes today's victim. Every person in the courtroom, including Antonia herself, is victim and victimizer, and accused and accuser, all at the same time. The practice of law is not about doing the right thing, but about doing the best thing under any given circumstances.

Antonia has become so cynical she is close to despair. She has seen life struggle from every conceivable perspective. It may seem that she can escape the cynicism in one of two ways. She can become completely self-absorbed with her own income and personal biases (which her inner integrity refuses to do). Or she can turn to politics and public policy (which her inner skepticism refuses to do). However, she does have a third alternative. She can escape cynicism by believing in the possibility of Kairos and the initiative of the infinite to give higher significance to life.

Antonia longs for a Last Word. Her life is lived in the midst of "temporary fixes" and "best alternatives" because a justice system can only react to the external mechanisms of cause and effect. The justice system can never alter the internal constitution of mind, heart, and relationship. She is aware that her own life stands under the same ultimate judgment as that of everyone else. She needs to experience Christ the Vindicator.

ECHO'S JOURNAL –

I am surprised that the mentor names his disciples so explicitly. It is unlikely that his audience will know them, yet he displays little concern for "confidentiality." I have begun to know these people in the give-and-take of our dialogues out there among the public. I wonder if they are offended?

The Chalcedonian Confession, as I understand it, is a product of Greek Christianity. Not Roman. It figures. Romans are like Americans—too rational, too controlling. They want God to be far too reasonable, and their obvious desire is for God to be ultimately controllable, manipulate-able, and manageable. Greek thinking is more subtle and mystical. I have an intuition that the terms Christ and Jesus have greater significance than I can comprehend right now—perhaps something historical and ancient.

The Cosmic Christ I can appreciate. I've already experienced the intervention of a "Higher Power," and now I can put a face to the abstraction. I've seen that Byzantine image staring down from the ceiling of the cathedral, the eyes boring down and through me to the depths of my being. It makes me shudder. It's not a "nice feeling" to be appraised by such a God.

I can appreciate the Vindicating Christ as well. Maybe I have never really felt the oppression of evil, as others might in the larger world; but we need some radical justice in the here and now.

It is Christ the Perfect Human that intrigues me. Perhaps it is this experience that is the most crucial one—and the most elusive one. Humanists have talked about being "truly human" for a long time. I've heard the phrase in so many innocuous, trite, obscure speeches from educators and politicians, but nobody seems to know what that actually means. And everybody seems to assume it is so easily attainable. Just one improved diet plan, charitable gift, or public policy away to be "truly human"!

What would that perfect human look like? Perfectly kind, perfectly fair, perfectly honest, perfectly balanced, perfectly wise, perfectly compassionate, perfectly reliable, perfectly approachable—it makes me think about the perfect woman I might marry and more. It makes me think of the perfect comrade in arms I might follow and more. Or the perfect friend to die for and more.

We usually settle for some approximation to perfection and think that imperfection is human as well. It makes us "lovable." Why wouldn't perfection be even more lovable? Nobody's perfect. But if nobody is perfect, how can we tell what is imperfect? If there is no original Mona Lisa smile, how can we tell which smiles are fakes?

We disciples gather again next week...

The Power and Depth of Being

At some point in my relationship with Mentor, I began trading e-mail with him. Unfortunately, one of those demonic computer viruses corrupted many of the files in my computer. I do not know when, where, or in what context this fragment was written....perhaps some convocation of philosophers or health care professionals, or part of a dialogue with students. He was such a peculiar person! For all I know, this is a byline from a Rock magazine.

The incarnation of Jesus the Christ is a personalization, localization, or paradigmatic representation of the great mystery of the intersection of the infinite and the finite. Our participation in this "intersection" is the hope that is intuited from the depths of existence and realized in existence only through the intervention of this Higher Power.

The Power of Being

The first three experiences of Jesus the Christ have been expressions of the power of being reaching into the depths of being. I use the term *Christ* to describe the divinity revealed in the incarnation.

- Christ is experienced in *Kairos*, radically changing our lives and turning life itself inside out and upside down, opening the possibility of a new beginning;

- Christ is experienced as *Logos*, the foundation of reason and the principle of order, structure, logic, and predictability in the universe;

- Christ is experienced as *Mythos*, the pattern of meaning that sets a standard of purpose and justice against which all human experience is measured.

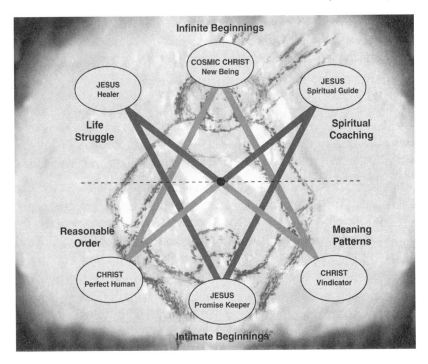

The "power of being" is that which lies beyond human control or comprehension, but which pervades and makes possible human control and comprehension.

The Depth of Being

I use the term *Jesus* to describe the second set of three experiences because these are expressions of the depth of being reaching outward in search of the power of being. The depth of being is that which lies within human control and comprehension, not just in mind, but in heart and soul as well. The depth of being can be expressed in science and innovation or in art and expression. The depth of being points toward and yearns for a higher form of Truth, Beauty, and Goodness.

- Jesus is experienced in the intimate beginnings of life, death, marriage, sex, and new creation, shaping the promise of what is to come.

- Jesus is experienced in the life struggles of suffering, toil, sickness, and insecurity, healing mind, body, emotion, relationship, and spirit.

- Jesus is experienced in the search for mentors who can guide us through the ethical ambiguities of personal and social history.

If there is value in the quest for the historical Jesus, it is here. The fullness of his humanity, of his historicity, is what allows the infinite to identify with existence by living in existence. It is what builds credibility and confidence for those in existence or trapped by existence to believe that God not only knows about our condition, but cares.

The Courage of Being

Christ the power of being and Jesus the depth of being reach across the plane of existence. Their unity, so to speak, is the empowerment of humanity for courage in life. This is more than mere knowledge (although insight is a part of empowerment). It is "en-courage-ment"…an embedding of radical courage by the Spirit.

- Cosmic Christ joins hands (so to speak) with Jesus the Promise Keeper, uniting infinite beginnings with intimate beginnings. We receive the courage to stand against the fundamental anxiety of fate and death. It is the courage to separate, create, stand apart, and be oneself. Identity, shattered or renewed, is the outcome of Kairos.

- Jesus the Spiritual Guide joins hands with Christ the Perfect Human, uniting the perfection of goodness, beauty, and truth with the quest to approximate it. We receive the courage to stand against the anxiety of emptiness and meaninglessness. It is the courage to participate, commit, stand with, and be a part. Trust, consistency, and predictability are the outcome of Logos.

- Jesus the Healer joins hands with Christ the Vindicator, uniting universal compassion with perfect justice. We receive the courage to stand against the anxiety of guilt and condemnation. It is the courage to accept and be accepted, and to accept our acceptance. Unity, meaningfulness, and purposefulness are the outcome of Mythos.

Encouragement (the experience of "having courage") is even more important than knowledge. Our knowledge will never be complete, but without courage we will never have the heart to endure existence in our search for knowledge …(here the manuscript is corrupted and incomplete).

ECHO'S JOURNAL _

Incarnation haunts me now. I see every human as an approximation of the divine and every experience as a partial revelation of Spirit. And I keep wondering what it would be like to encounter a concrete person who is not approximation, but the real thing, the full and complete revelation of Spirit. What would be the result of such an encounter?

I sit in the bakery café following our last conversation with the mentor. Everyone is gone, but the aroma of fresh bread fills the room and bids me stay. "Fresh bread"—another oxymoron, like "new being." There really is no such thing as "fresh" bread, because the very moment the bread is taken from the oven and begins to cool, it is no longer "fresh." Its "freshness" progresses at an accelerated pace toward staleness, mold, and disintegration. The claim that the bread is "fresh" is at best an exaggeration. It is simply bread in the early stages of staleness.

This is just like our existence. I am not really alive, but only in the early stages of dying. Next week when I have coffee here, I may have cancer; the following week I may only eat the bread and skip the coffee from nausea; the next week I may be dead. Who knows? Even the newborn baby, "fresh from the oven" (as it were), is not "fresh" but already in process toward staleness. Morbid thinking, perhaps, but in fact an ancient awe.

It is the aroma of baking, not the taste of pastry, that sets me to yearning for fresh bread. The bread comes and goes, but the aroma endures. It's like a promise awaiting fulfillment. The mentor's "new being" is like this. It is not the creature itself, but the aroma of being that is ever-new and ever-fresh. If Logos were the structure of the oven itself, and Mythos were flour and yeast, and Kairos were the heat of the fire, together they would create an aroma that would make you salivate for the infinite.

Imagine a magic bread, presented with all the pride the chef can muster. It is not bread as we know it. It is the concreteness, the distillation, the essence itself of the freshness of bread. Eating it will bring a satisfaction normal bread cannot provide. Imagine a person who is not a person, yet one who is the concreteness of new being itself—the aroma of the infinite, but able to sit and converse at this very table where I sit now. There is so much I would want to ask, but I suspect I would be too awestruck for speech, and speech would seem so inadequate. And if I did have cancer, would I be healed? Or would it even matter anymore?

SEVENTH MENTORING MOMENT

The Experience of Jesus

The experience of yearning is itself a spiritual experience. One might say that religion is part of the internal constitution of existence. It cannot be explained away as a psychological compulsion or a cultural phenomenon or an intellectual category mistake. It is more like the instinct to return "home" for migratory animals or the desire for companionship and procreation. It is an "urge," or better yet, an "urgency" about living that strains toward something deeper, higher, purer, and lasting.

If the experience of Christ is the infinite responding *in general* to the predicament of existence, then the experience of Jesus is the infinite responding *in particular* to the yearning of the individual person. It is God emerging from the depth of being itself and not simply intruding from beyond being itself. Incarnation is the reunion of God with God, which brings existence along in its wake. It is as if Christ were a great wave crashing upon the shore of our lives, followed by a powerful "undertow" as the water recedes back into the ocean dragging all the flotsam and jetsam of existence along with it.

Yet this metaphor still fails to express the intentionality, urgency, and compassion with which the infinite responds to finite yearning. The wave is customized to crash upon *my* life, erode *my* resistance, and draw *my* existence toward the infinite in a manner that will address *my* deepest yearning. God reaches not only toward, but also through, my very heart to bring hope. This "gut wrenching" is the Spirit shattering my sense of well-being, harmony, and contentment. The struggle, pain, brokenness; the ambiguity, doubt, and uncertainty—all this provokes a desperation and awakens a desire to be reunited with the infinite.

48

Experiencing Jesus the Promise Keeper

Jesus the Promise Keeper is not only within the comprehension of human imagination, but represents the epitome of human want and yearning. Jesus is the Expected One, the one whose arrival the prophets and seers and mystics keep predicting. He is the one you really expect to walk through the door—in the next minute, hour, or lifetime. He is the Faithful One, the Ground of All Hope, and the Messiah. He is the Source of Vision, the Dreamer of the First Dream, the Guarantee of Rescue. He is the True Vine, into which perishable organisms may be grafted for new life. He is the Sustainer, the Encourager, the Intercessor, the Upholder, and the Enduring Hope.

In the midst of labor pains for new babies, new relationships, new communities, and new dreams, Jesus the Promise Keeper, stretches out to prepare for the struggle of life. The best way to equip new creations for the real world is not to teach them knowledge and skills that will become obsolete. The best way is not to burden them with obligations and inheritances that will make them feel guilty. The best way is to provide them with the wisest and most visionary spiritual guides you can find. Jesus the Promise Keeper is the guarantor of covenants. The way to survive life struggle is not to find all the answers to life's questions, but to live in a trustworthy companionship with people who can help you on your way.

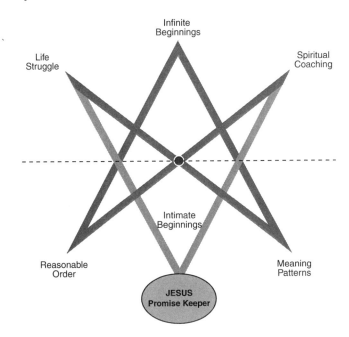

The single most important covenant is the promise to "come again." It is this expectation—that love can come again, or that hope can come again, or that joy can come again—that ultimately rescues us from despair and suicide. This conviction that the New Being can "come again" is what makes all other promises somehow believable.

The depth of being is really a pattern of interlocking promises—promises to spouses, children or parents, friends and enemies, employers and employees, governments, organizations, charities, and religious institutions. Vows are made with daily commitments and lifelong implications. Yet life is really a pattern of *broken* promises—divorce, alienation, benefits denied, rights ignored, generosity abused, and commitments forgotten. In a world of incredible cynicism and skepticism, people long to long for reassurance.

Guilt and shame comprise the hot, shifting magma that has replaced solid earth at the foundation of our lives. Guilt has more to do with moral transgression and the breaking of covenants of fidelity. It is the conscience that disturbs us when our family is not honored, or the hungry are not fed, or friendships are not preserved. Shame, however, has more to do with personal uncleanness. It is the knowledge of unworthiness, the intuition of a more profound defilement that has sullied our reputation and self-esteem. Jesus the Promise Keeper, is the assurance of a deeper forgiveness and cleansing. Intimate beginnings anticipate, and point toward, infinite beginnings.

Promise Keeping Now

Debra K. is a teacher specializing in English literature with a long career in secondary public school education. Now the principal of a large suburban school, she stands at the center of all the stress surrounding educational standards, emerging learning methodologies, local and state politics, and ethical issues that trouble the minds of cynical teens. Innumerable ambiguities and difficult challenges have invaded her life, but one thing is constant and clear: Her career and her lifestyle—her work and her life—have merged.

- Debra cannot separate the pain and joy she experienced giving birth to her own children from the pain and joy she experiences helping children and youth birth their inner potential.

- Debra cannot separate the enjoyment of dining out with her life partner from interested engagement with the youthful waiter who is a former student from years ago.

- Debra cannot separate her anxiety for her own future and that of her family from her anxiety for the future of her students (an extended family) in an increasingly violent world and polluted environment.

The stress in Debra's life has been building and building, as racking as the pains of labor in the birthing room but with less hope of a happy ending. Her doctor has warned her that unless she more clearly differentiates her private life from her work life, she will burn out. She has toyed with early retirement. Yet she can't do it. She thinks there must be something more, some fruit yet to be born, and some mentoring relationship yet to be brokered for her school of seekers. Yet as time goes by, she herself becomes increasingly cynical. Her world is increasingly a world of broken promises and unfulfilled dreams that compromise her integrity.

Debra longs for a new start, a rebirth, and a second chance. Yet her longing is for more than that. She also longs for a satisfactory conclusion, and unchanging intimacy, and a final consummation. She does not want to be on a journey in life unless there is a destination for life. She does not require simple answers or a handful of steps toward success. She can accept ambiguities, endure trials, and meet challenges, *if there is confidence that the entire ordeal will be worth it.*

Experiencing Jesus the Healer

As long as nature itself is subverted by decay and human nature itself is tainted by selfishness, people will yearn for a supernatural intervention that can break the laws of science and transform the habits of humankind. Jesus is the Reconciler, the Compassionate One, and the Eraser of Sins. He is the Gift Giver, the Angel of Mercy, and the Touch of God. Jesus is the Peace Maker, the Serenity Bringer, the Sea Calmer. He is the Body Builder and the Mind Mender, the Soul Seeker and the Heart Healer.

In the midst of life struggle, Jesus the Healer stretches out to connect with our need. Insofar as the experience of Jesus is a response to our need, the experience emerges from the depth of being (from "below"). Yet insofar as the divine response initiates new beginnings and fresh patterns of meaning, the experience emerges from the power of being (from "above"). The healing touch is perhaps the most powerful experience of intimacy, but it demands interpretation to invest it with meaning and purpose.

Life struggle is an experience of brokenness, fragmentation, or alienation. It is not just the inevitability of death but the immanence of death that accelerates panic, anxiety, and fear. True healing involves more than curing a disease, restoring a relationship, or fending off starvation for another day, though it cannot ignore the importance of these things as a step on the way. Practical intervention depends on the fulfillment of promises or covenants that bind people together, but long-term healing demands justice at the end of time.

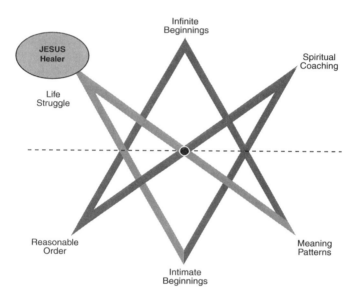

Healing can be physical, mental, emotional, relational, or spiritual. It is holistic. The import of healing is that it leads to both meaning patterns and intimate beginnings. The "next step," so to speak, in any experience of healing is to develop a "mythology" or a pattern of meaning with which to interpret the experience. Such a pattern of meaning helps the individual express gratitude, celebrate joy, and communicate the hope of welcome relief to others. In addition, the individual can move to an acceptance of self, others, and God that allows him or her to leave the past behind and make a fresh start in life.

Healing Now

Maria S. is a surgeon in the cardiology unit of a major hospital. The struggle for life is an everyday occurrence in her profession. She readily tells stories such as the following:

- A patient is admitted for quadruple heart bypass surgery for which he has waited months in relative immobility. The combination of new technology and medical expertise gives the patient his life back.
- Another person undergoes emergency surgery for an aortic aneurism. So severe is the trauma to such an elderly person that doctors give up hope and call the family and the priest for the last rites. As the family mutters the Lord's Prayer, her vital signs stabilize, and days later she is discharged in good health.
- A single mother is admitted experiencing chest pain and beside herself with anxiety. She is later diagnosed with severe gall stones and undergoes a relatively simple operation. Yet the crisis reshapes her relationships and lifestyle.

The issue is never through whose hands or with what technologies healing happens. It is still an intersection of the infinite and the finite. Maria understands this, but more importantly, she can coach her patients into the next steps. She can help them develop a mythology—a meaning pattern—with which to interpret the experience. And she can help them reexamine their intimacy with self, others, and God to make a fresh start in life.

Maria knows that more is wrong with the human condition than a hospital can cure. Indeed, she knows that as long as the deeper brokenness of the human spirit remains unhealed, the hospitals and emergency rooms and clinics of the world will continue to be full. She cannot ignore the unexplainable cancer remissions or the dramatic improvements in mental health or the tearful reconciliations of long estranged enemies. She has stopped looking for scientific interpretations for every unexpectedly positive turnabout. But dare she believe that there is something more personal and intentional about these healings than mere, dumb, random good fortune? And dare she imagine that there is a deeper, primordial experience of healing going on that may be visible in the body yet reach deeper into the soul? Does she need to experience Jesus the Healer?

Experiencing Jesus the Spiritual Guide

Information floods—nay swamps—our lives, but the wisdom to interpret information and apply it for the improvement of ourselves and the world is in short supply. Many can analyze information, but few can synthesize it. Jesus is the Mentor. He is the Soul Searcher, the Lifestyle Shaper, the Fog Clearer, and the Truth Teller. He is the Pilgrim Leader, Sage, Magi, Elder, and Wise One. He is the Story Teller, the Gatherer, the Model, and the Discerner of Meaning. He is Midwife to our spirits, and Pathfinder to our search. He speaks the Good Word at the Right Time.

Our need for good advice, personal support, and wise guidance has increased exponentially as daily living becomes more and more complex. In the midst of all the advice, counseling, and therapy that we receive for health, happiness, and fulfillment, Jesus the Spiritual Guide stretches out as the mentor for life purpose and joy.

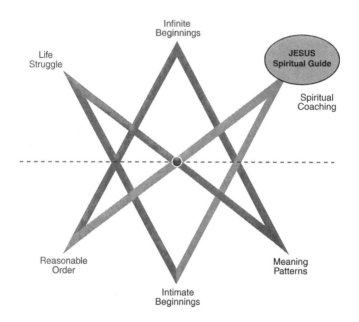

Every founder of a great religion spent most of his or her time mentoring a handful of disciples. Jesus was no exception. Mentoring is a form of teaching, but is accomplished in parables, analogies, stories, conversation, and behavior modeling as well as exposition, abstraction, analysis, and meditation. Mentoring is more comprehensive and also more informal than teaching. It happens spontaneously, out of the depth of experience and wisdom of the mentor, in response to whatever opportunity or circumstance emerges in life. It also happens daringly, out of the mentor's life struggle and experience of God, in response to particular challenges or crises in life. Mentors are neither born nor created. They are called and developed. For Christians, Jesus is the preeminent mentor, the person one most wishes to spend time with in conversation.

Although mentoring happens in many ways, the goal of mentoring is quite clear. It is primarily behavioral, rather than merely theoretical. It aims at shaping a lifestyle to endow it with integrity and credibility. Mentors help people reorder their lives to clearly align with the values, convictions, and purpose that lie at the heart of each individual. Mentoring is also primarily about creating the new, rather than maintaining the old. The intimacy of the mentoring relationship is not a cocoon, but is intended to precipitate new projects, new missions, new ideas, and new directions. True mentoring leads to innovation.

Mentoring Now

Calvin H. is a social worker associated with the mental health and child welfare programs of an urban development. He spends enormous amounts of time connecting individuals and families with social programs, and is increasingly frustrated that so few lives really break out of the cycle of social, economic, and educational traps in which his clients find themselves. Calvin notices two things:

- His clients need something more comprehensive, and more continuous, than the hodgepodge of federal, state, and local programs that are politically precarious and chronically underbudgeted. It's *not* that they need a church! And he wouldn't ever recommend merely institutional religion! But Calvin senses that his people need a more fundamental and holistic kind of coaching that will help them not just put their family, health, or budget back together, but put *life* back together. They need a life coach, not just a case worker, who can help them bring order to the chaos and birth a clean, fresh start.

- He personally needs a clarity of mission that is more than the vague philanthropic compassion that got him into social work in the first place. The high-sounding words that used to motivate him just don't cut it anymore in the real world of few results, big bureaucracy, and low pay. He feels fragmented by a thousand programs, but without an overarching purpose with which he can measure real success. If his clients are looking for coaching, so is he. But all the conferences, professional literature, self-help books, and networks of chain-smoking and caffeine-addicted friends can't provide it.

Calvin is not looking for therapy. Nor is he looking for just the right political coalition that promises to deliver the just society. He is looking for someone who can awaken, touch, direct, and coach the spirit, his spirit and that of his many clients. Such a coach could help bring a synthesis to life, a purpose to living, and a rebirth of his original passion for the wellness of others.

Incarnation happens as the intersection of the infinite and the finite defines our plane of existence. It is God experienced under the conditions of real life and the actual passage of time, or actual existence as it is lived under the irrevocable limitation of death. Therefore, the truth of Christ lies not in dogmatic statements or theological summaries, but in the experience itself. Experience means encounter that is at once relational, emotional, and physical as well as spiritual and intellectual.

Incarnation is not a noun. It is not a state of being, but a process of becoming. One might better say that God is being incarnated over and over again as the complexity of life intersects the complexity of God in unpredictable ways. The individual is drawn into that incarnation, becomes part of that incarnational moment. If God becomes "present" to the world and to our own personal corner of that world, so also do we become "present" to heaven and to our own personal corner of that heaven. Christ becomes the talisman (symbol to the depth of being and portal to the power of being) that makes such incarnation possible for us.

ECHO'S JOURNAL _

I asked the individuals in our group if they were offended when the mentor named them as examples of people in a spiritual quest. They all looked rather puzzled, as if being offended was something that had never really occurred to them. "Of course," I thought. "What real seeker would be offended by being associated with a spiritual quest?" I suddenly realized what these "disciples" around me are really willing to "stake" for the quest. They risk careers, relationships, stability, and even the semblance of "normality" that so many people today draw over their heads like a blanket on a stormy night.

I have begun to use the journaling process that the mentor has been teaching—pondering the position of my soul on the talisman of the star. There have been times in my life when I have struggled desperately against brokenness, disease, and the threat of death; and I know what comfort and encouragement I found as patterns of meaning drew me out of my hurt toward vindication and healing.

It did not take long, however, before I found myself once again "uncentered," lost in the fog of doubt and ethical ambiguity. Whether this was the doing of culture or Spirit, I cannot say. Perhaps both/and? My yearning is for spiritual guidance, and I suppose that is why I am here, talking with a mentor who is often obscure, but always relevant.

If I look across the star diagram for the magnetism that will draw me back to my "centered" self, I realize that there is a method of thought and answers to be found; and while I may be guided in the right direction, it is up to me to discern the answers.

I have growing confidence that I can find the truth. My greater anxiety is that I will not be able to accept the truth. My selfishness may get in the way, or my addictions may get in the way. Perhaps the more I move to the center, the more vulnerable I will become to the intrusion of intimate beginnings that will challenge my selfishness—or infinite beginnings that will shatter my addictions.

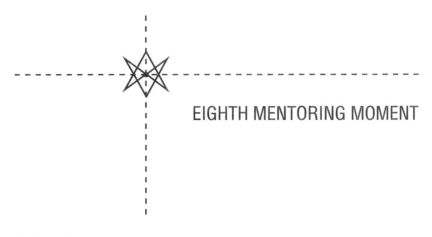

EIGHTH MENTORING MOMENT

Worship

Worship in any religion is the convergence of the infinite and the finite, shaped by the personal disciplines and mentoring relationships of participants. It is the plane or horizon caused by the intersection of Kairos into the Logos and Mythos that shapes our being-in-the-world.

Experiencing the Eternal Now

For Christians, this intersection of the infinite and the finite is defined by the paradigm of Christ. It is that poignant moment when the divine and the human Jesus converge into a single experience, bridging the gap between divine and human. Worship is the synchronous expression of that "eternal now" as the Eucharist is celebrated as the body and blood and as the spirit and fullness of God, in a single ritual.

This intersection of the finite and the infinite is the plane of our existence. The eternal now is chaos—a constantly bubbling, boiling cauldron of unpredictable heat, depth, and magnitude, in which continuities emerge and dissipate, reliable social structures rise and fall, perspectives attract a following and then dissolve again. Yet the eternal now is also Logos—a constant, abiding, calm, unchanging, single, incarnate experience of love and acceptance. If the finite and infinite were separate and never intersected, there would be neither chaos, nor redemption. Incarnation, classically understood, is the intersection of the fully human and the fully divine, which simultaneously provokes change and assures hope.

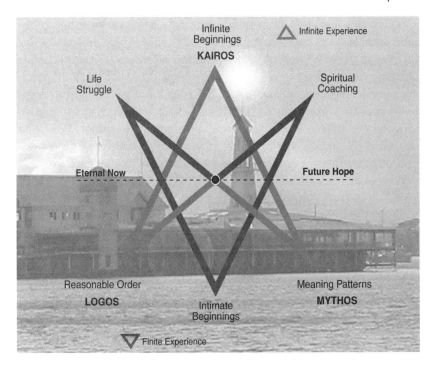

If Antonia worships at all, it will not be in a typical Protestant church with all of its wordiness and routine. She has no interest in cross-generational children's stories, and the sermons seem insipid and pointless compared to the life-and-death drama of the courtroom. She chooses to worship only on special high holy days of the year (Christmas and Easter, sacraments of Eucharist, Adult Baptism, Ordination, and Unction), and most likely in ancient languages, with unaccompanied musical voices and high drama. She does not seek to test her mind, but to exercise her soul. She needs to see, hear, smell, and taste the incarnation in order to have hope beyond the damnation she sees over and again in the justice system.

No single liturgy or ritual can grasp what is essentially a nonrational experience of the eternal now. Worship is a mystical experience of unity or merging, and any particular structure or symbolism for worship is at best an approximation or an aid toward that experience.

Therefore, the most significant influences to shape worship are *not* heritage, scholarship, or culture, but rather the spiritual discipline of the believer and the mentoring relationships in which the believer participates.

Worship that does not emerge from the spiritual discipline of the individual is mere form and empty ritual. It may still be *meaningful,* but its meaning is only tied to the preservation of history, the protection of culture, or the transference of knowledge. In short, it is a merely sociological meaningfulness. In fact, this is all the modern anthropologist really sees in worship, and it is all the government values in worship. As long as worship is separated from the primary shaping of spiritual discipline, the world's representative governments, educational institutions, and corporate bodies can shape worship to achieve its own ends to coerce and mold public attitudes.

Worship that does emerge from spiritual discipline, however, readies itself for the in-breaking of Kairos. It is a climate of spiritual waiting, an environment in which the nonrational can simultaneously employ and shatter whatever liturgies, rites, educational assumptions, and other structures might be used. Once the desire for God, the readiness to receive the spirit, or the yearning for the infinite is present in the hearts of the worshipers, then God can invade, inspire, enthrall, and otherwise impact the world in unpredictable ways. For this reason, governments, educational institutions, and other corporate bodies *fear* true worship, because they cannot contain or control it. True worship lies forever beyond the sociologist's grasp.

> Wally S. is not a spiritually disciplined person. He attends worship occasionally when he has nothing else to do or when his children are performing in some role. Worship is a supplement to the public school system and to a community service club, a vehicle for the socialization of himself and his family. There is comfort in acceptance and membership privilege—and that alone is worth fighting to protect, worth serving on the board to preserve—but nothing more. Wally would be more than confused if God invaded, enthralled, inspired, and impacted the worship rites in unpredictable ways. He would be offended.

Worship that does not emerge from relationships of mutual mentoring is mere therapy and aesthetic experience. It may still be *meaningful,* but its meaning is only tied to subjective needs, personal prejudices, or artistic preferences. In short, it is merely psychological meaningfulness. This is all the modern psychologist sees in worship, and it is all the cultural community values in worship. As long as worship is separated from the primary shaping of mentoring relationships (a "community of spiritually disciplined people" or a "body of Christ"), musicians' guilds and mental health clinics can shape worship as a concert venue or cathartic experience.

Worship that does emerge from a body of mutual mentoring, however, carries an implicit humility before the Holy. A constant critique of individual need and desire, expectation and prejudice, has already unfolded to ensure that worship is not about "me," "my needs," or "my preferences," but rather about "God," "the needs of the world," and "our hopes." This is only possible if there is constant accountability for the mutual encouragement, challenge, and support of the community that gathers to worship. Revelation, inspiration, and apocalyptic change can be interpreted and focused by the mutual mentoring of those on a parallel path of self-discipline. For this reason musicians' guilds and mental health clinics *fear* true worship, because they lose their power to judge it as "good" worship or "bad" worship.

> Debra K. is committed to information assimilation and the expansion of every person's individual databank. She is not interested in lifestyle mentoring, nor does she fully understand it. She attends worship regularly, demands exceptionally high quality expository preaching, and weighs every word of the ritual for substance and political correctness. Worship is for her a means to educate people in good music, good diction, respectful behavior, and moral thinking. Control is best exercised not in the children's classroom, but in the worship and personnel committees, because together this is the fulcrum on which life turns. Debra would not only be confused if worship were to become indigenous, unpleasant, or unpredictable. She would be offended.

The irony is that what governments, institutions, guilds, and clinics fear is precisely what individual government workers, teachers, musicians, and psychologists may personally welcome. However meaningful worship might be separated from spiritual discipline and mutual mentoring, these individuals know that the institutional purposes of worship are an essential hypocrisy. The sociological, psychological, and aesthetic purposes of worship are judged and shattered by the real experience of the eternal now.

The eternal now is a mystical moment that assumes—or better still, is passionately confident—that an infinite experience exists beyond finite experience and that infinite experience is not indifferent to finite experience. The eternal now is made possible by this dual interest of the infinite and the finite in each other. The infinite seeks to fulfill itself and its purposes in and through the finite, and the finite yearns to reunite with the infinite. Worship is the culmination of that twin desire.

Worship as the eternal now is not motivated by Agape or Phileos—neither by sacrificial love nor loving fellowship—but by Eros. The passionate, creative, longing hunger for fulfillment is the depth dimension of true worship. Its fruit is not philanthropic stewardship, nor is it friendly relationships, but absolute dedication to shape lifestyle around mission. Worship precipitates mission, because mission is the only way God can fulfill history on the one hand, and the only way individuals can satisfy their hunger to be perfectly synchronized with infinite purpose.

The "legion of the lapsed" hold all so-called church worship in varying degrees of contempt. This contempt may be very polite; it may be expressed by deliberate absence or general indifference rather than by articulate critique or violent objection. Usually this contempt is disguised by appealing to other issues that critics know will appeal to the sociologists and psychologists of religion or to the aesthetes and professional liturgists of the institution. The disguised criticism of the church is designed to throw religious leaders off the scent, because the legion of the lapsed have long given up any hope in talking to them. The strategy works very well, because institutional religious leaders and institutional religious commentators immediately isolate themselves from the public to hold conferences, write papers, and attend conventions in which they vigorously debate among themselves and never engage the real intersection of the infinite and the finite.

"Worship is too boring," they say, which sidetracks the discussion away from the real exploration of worship as the eternal now into stylistic debates over musical genre, performance, and entertainment. What the legion of the lapsed really want to say is that institutional worship in North America is never really apocalyptic. It is never really about infinite beginnings, never an in-breaking of Kairos that changes life (my life, your life, our life, somebody's life) forever. Even in supposedly "Pentecostal" churches people merely speak in tongues and go home to lunch. It is not that the process of worship is too boring, but that the results of worship are too boring. The radical Eros of the infinite never makes love to anyone or makes anyone pregnant with the potentialities of the divine.

> Bill J. frequently finds worship boring, regardless of its style. He enjoys inspiration. He longs for opportunities to make his heart race, experiences to make his heart sing, or sights and sounds that move him to tears. He knows that he can experience such inspiration more powerfully, and without the guilt load and financial overhead of the institutional church, if he has season

tickets to the opera and occasionally goes to Las Vegas. Yet even then, Bill intuits that such inspiration is short-term at best. It takes him out of his corporate world for moments of refreshment, but it does not really change his corporate world. He longs for more than inspiration. He longs for an apocalypse.

"Worship is irrelevant," they say, which sidetracks the discussion away from the real exploration of worship as the eternal now into ideological debates over political advocacy, career coaching, family nurture, and personal therapy. What the legion of the lapsed really want to say is that institutional worship in North America is never profoundly fulfilling. It is never about intimate beginnings, never a passionate touch with an outstretched heart that leaves the worshiper gasping for breath, saying, "Now, at last, if this were my last moment of life, I could die in peace." Even in supposedly sacramental churches, people are merely confirmed in their routines and rarely make a clear, fresh start. The radical Eros of the finite never extends itself into the unknown or readies anyone for new being.

> Calvin H. frequently finds worship irrelevant, no matter what its ideological position, because it simply does not lead anywhere. He yearns for worship that is just as results driven as his everyday life. Either change a life or change the world, but for God's sake change something! He needs to see a missional "product" at the end of all that ritual. The oratory of Saint Bernard would have gone right to his heart, because that worship launched a crusade. The mass rallies of George Whitfield would have caught his imagination, because that worship helped foment a revolution. The house churches of the Wesleyan movement would have drawn him like a magnet, because that worship inspired economic justice for the working class.

The legion of the lapsed deliberately sidetrack conversation with institutionally religious leaders about worship because they have become convinced that despite all the conferences, conventions, and cosmetic changes to institutional worship, institutional leaders do not want worship to be anything but boring and irrelevant. Boring, irrelevant worship is precisely what governments, educational institutions, scientific bodies, health care plans, sociological research foundations, and denominations want. Then it can be managed and controlled. It can be used to generate reliable incomes for clergy, manipulate public opinion, and embed social habits and politically correct cultural mores. It can be yet another social program directed by experts for rational ends. Yet as cynical as the legion of the lapsed have become, they *know* that there is another kind of worship—worship as the eternal now. On occasion, they have experienced it. Often unexpectedly, they have participated in it. They have heard colleagues whisper about it. They have met spiritual leaders ("professional" or "amateur") who are encouraging it. They know it is possible.

Worship as the eternal now emerges from the serious spiritual discipline of leaders and participants. It is not diversion from their lifestyle, but a product of their lifestyle. It is the culmination of an intentionally oriented, countercultural behavior pattern that they have practiced through the week at work and at leisure, alone and with friends and family. It emerges from credible people who obsessively model a peculiar set of shared values and who habitually turn to an articulate set of convictions to give them strength in evil times.

> Debra K. may be tempted back to an experience of worship if it becomes an experience of the eternal now. If she senses God to be "present" to her existence and simultaneously senses herself to be "present" to God, she will feel the impact of worship permeating her leadership in public education and influencing her mentoring among students and teachers. She will experience companionship in a counterculture. She will be mentored in order to mentor. She will be spiritually guided in order to become a spiritual guide. She will model alternative core values, but this time with the reasonable hope that education can be enhanced by the mystical movement of the Spirit.

Worship as the eternal now is linked to a larger process of mutual mentoring and support. It motivates a discipline that can make life meaningful and rescue it from despair, can bring order to chaos and prevent giving in to the temptation of suicide. It is an absolute surrender of self-centeredness, a community made possible solely by incarnation and nothing else. Life-on-the-edge and life-in-between can merge into life-at-peace.

> Maria S. may be tempted back to an experience of worship if it becomes an experience of the eternal now. If she senses that God's healing power is not rendering her efforts trivial but rather infusing her efforts for a more comprehensive wellness of a human life with real hope for success, she will immerse herself in worship with the passion of a fanatic. Worship can justify her self-sacrifice and give her strength to endure constant stress. But

more importantly, she can make life-and-death decisions in the confidence that they are existentially relative to an absolute decision for "life" that has already been made and that is (thankfully) beyond her control.

It *is* possible. They believe in the paradox that there is a plane of intersection, a state of being, in which the divine can be incarnate and people can participate directly with the infinite. They know that the infinite is *not* neutral to the finite. They know that no matter how much institutional religion seeks to block the intersection of the infinite and finite, the infinite will *invade* the finite; and the finite will *reach out* to the infinite, shattering all pretense of order, management, and control. The Kairos will happen, and the new being *will* emerge, because nothing can stop the combined Eros of God and the human spirit.

ECHO'S JOURNAL _

Personally, I was raised as a Christian but gave up on Christian worship long ago. It wasn't that I was any less desirous of meeting God. If anything, I wanted to meet God above all things. And that is precisely why I dropped out of worship. The worship at the churches I knew only introduced me to heritages, structures, ideologies, dogmas, duties, trivialities, personalities, conflicts, and debates that always sidetracked my quest for God. The tactics and by-products of worship sabotaged worship for me.

The mentor presented this speech as a kind of sermon in the chapel of a seminary. I and a few of our group attended, feeling like outsiders and treated as such by the glances and frowns of the faculty, students, and other churchy people, body language that belied their hospitable coffee. The response was a mixture of boredom, befuddlement, and anger. They all seemed so quick to debate the tactics of worship, making hasty assumptions about sanctuaries, liturgies, music, leadership, and so on. What is the phrase I remember from Sunday school? "Straining out gnats and swallowing camels"?

The "eternal now" is another of a seemingly endless series of oxymora that permeate the teaching of the mentor. It makes no more sense to them than "new being," "incarnation," and other phrases, and yet makes perfect sense to us. That worship should be an experience of timelessness or an intersection of the infinite and finite in a particular space and particular time is true to my own moments of insight or revelation. Why anyone would demand that the eternal now be standardized, uniformly experienced, and franchised among institutions boggles my mind.

I suppose it comes back to the issue of control. The plane of the eternal now is, after all, the result of the vertical intersection of the infinite and the finite—not the horizontal intersection of spiritual guides (preachers) and mythologies (liturgies), with life struggles (therapies) and reasonable order (institutions). It's as if religion has been skewed ninety degrees—whether to the "left" or "right" doesn't matter; it's skewed.

What impressed me most about the mentor's view of worship is that it is really not a manageable experience at all. One can't really plan for it, design it, or direct it. Yet I think it would be wrong to think that it simply "happens," anywhere, anytime, to anyone, regardless of expectation. I think "expectation" is the crucial ingredient. The yearning from the depth of being becomes so intense and the conviction in the power of being becomes so strong that the atmosphere becomes electric, poignant, ready, filled with anticipation for God knows what.

NINTH MENTORING MOMENT

Life in the Spirit

Life should be worth living. It must be more than a chronology of years and a sequence of life cycles. It must be an existence. If it is to be an existence, then life must be lived in various forms of communion with the infinite. There must be hope. We intuitively understand that the quest for a worthwhile life is more than an intellectual exercise, or a passive process of meditation, or an active support of good causes, or a healthy experience of family, or a personal sense of well-being. Life is all of these, of course, but it is more. Life must be lived in connection with all six experiences of Christ and with the courageous confidence to risk everything for higher purposes. Life must be lived in the wisdom to endure ambiguous choices in the serenity of ultimate acceptance. My mentor called this "Life in the Spirit."[1]

This life in the spirit entails six necessities. We see these echoed in all ancient and contemporary religions. They were a part of the identity of Israel in the Torah and of the renewal of covenant proclaimed by the prophets. They were a part of the original Christian community described in the Acts of the Apostles. They were most clearly defined in the "rules" of the first monasteries and nunneries.

- A focus for meditation
- A pilgrim band for participation
- A mentoring relationship for concentration
- An ordered life for cooperation
- A missional purpose for a stranger's salvation
- An ultimate hope for creation's final destination.

Tactics may differ. Theologies may diverge. Terminologies may change. The language of Jesus the Christ and the traditions of the Christian movement have obviously been decisive for my pursuit of life in the spirit and for that of my mentors. The basic components of life in the spirit are the same.

The Focus of Meditation

This focus is a practical, visible, tactile tool that helps individuals focus their thoughts and center their hearts. It is the talisman itself (as described in the preface). It is a symbol that reminds and instructs, and it is a portal through which the infinite probes and guides. The graphic image of the six-pointed star is such a talisman. Behind the graphic can be placed the changing images (pictures) that from time to time, and from Kairos moment to Kairos moment, seize our attention and expand our imagination. We hold the talisman in front of ourselves as the devotional object for meditation. It is the screen saver on our computer to remind us of where we are and where we are going. It is dangling from our rearview mirror to align us with purpose in the midst of busy living. It is an icon on our wall to channel our thoughts and resist the temptations for distraction beyond.

Yet another focus for meditation will be introduced shortly. It is my version of the rosary. This devotional object of beads and necklace, ordered to guide our meditation and portable for use in church or on the run, in joy or in sorrow, is a practical tool for meditation. Traditional tools have included the Stations of the Cross for Catholics and the biblical lectionary for Protestants; or meditations on the Koran and pilgrimage to Mecca for Muslims; or phylacteries, daily rituals, and dress for Jews; or bells, dances, postures, and images for many religions. The rationalized West trivializes such foci for meditation at best and fears them as false "idolatries" at worst. Yet they become increasingly important in order to center ourselves on the life in the spirit.

A Pilgrim Band for Participation

The pilgrim band is a small group, cell, or "traveling companionship" for the spiritual journey. These are your comrades in the spiritual struggle against temptation and your support group to align your life to shared ultimate concern. This peer group of friends helps you find yourself on the talisman map of the spiritual life. They help you understand your life when it is "on-the-edge" and requires courage, or is "in-between" and requires wisdom, or is "at-peace" and experiences serenity. They help you anticipate the next challenge and move strategically amid change.

They hold you accountable for personal growth and, at times, for mere endurance.

The technique of participation is a spiritual exercise often called "journaling," but this term misleads people into thinking it is a form of diary. This is not an individual exercise. It does not recount the events of the day and it is not intended to recapture your past. This is a corporate or group exercise that sharpens your perception of the finite intersecting with the finite, discerns Jesus the Christ incarnate in your life, and focuses your personal mission into the future. The basic elements of the spiritual exercise are:

- *Christ as we find him:* Which of the six experiences of Jesus the Christ (Cosmic Christ, Vindicator, Perfect Human...Promise Keeper, Healer, or Spiritual Guide) are most real to your current experience?
- *Life as we know it:* What is your position amid the six points of existence (infinite beginnings, meaning patterns, reasonable order...intimate beginnings, life struggle, spiritual coaching), and in what sense is your life "on-the-edge," "in-between," or "at-peace"?
- *Mission as we see it:* What is your personal mission, the pursuit of which unites you with God and the fulfillment of which gives your life significance?
- *God as he wants us:* What are the next steps, strategic moves, courageous acts, or personal risks that will take you closer to God or place you squarely in God's way?

The exercise itself is presented as an appendix at the end of this book and is used in combination with my version of the rosary as a focus for meditation.

The talisman itself (the star diagram depicting the six points of existence and the six experiences of Jesus the Christ) is the primary focus of the "pilgrim band." They can place any image or picture *behind* the talisman that currently captures their imagination and focuses their conversation. For example, the talisman on page 28 is set against a photo of the Golden Gate Bridge because that image of the bridge emerging from the fog captured my attention as a symbol of the intersection between the infinite and the finite. It emerges clearly from the mists and confusion of existence and disappears as readily, but for that moment it is incarnate, or present to my experience. The bridge itself was the Christ Experience, and its sight was an act of worship. In the "eternal now" that made me oblivious of all the chaos of life around me, Christ addressed me as the Promise Keeper and opened an intimate beginning to a new chapter of my spiritual journey.

At another time, another place, and another existential position in the spiritual journey, one might use another image (still photo, video clip, sound byte, or object) that functions as a background to the talisman. That, too, can be visually or experientially shared with one's "pilgrim band" to help them understand and reflect and guide the individual into the next steps of the spiritual journey. The image that follows was taken along the Great Ocean Drive in southern Australia near the outcrops known as "The Twelve Apostles."

The turgid water rushing in and out of the narrow gap between two rock outcrops and the noise and salt spray that overwhelmed the senses seized my attention as the intersection of the infinite and the finite. Beyond lies nothing but the fathomless ocean until frigid Antarctica; behind seems a fragile existence eroded by the passage of time and the sudden in-breaking of God. God bursts in between the reasonable order and patterns of meaning in our existence to create…what? Here the Cosmic Christ, the apocalyptic one, is revealed, and the future is suddenly unpredictable. It would be better as a video and sound clip. The pilgrim band could understand my life position better and help me discern the next steps in the spiritual journey.

A Mentoring Relationship for Concentration

Mentors help people discern and clarify their personal mission. They are not therapists, although from time to time they may calm emotions.

They are not teachers, although from time to time they may instruct the mind. They are not activists, although from time to time they may model moral behavior. Everything a mentor does is designed to help others discern their calling, pursue their calling, and accomplish their calling. They help people find their way in the search for the infinite or open their lives to the coming of the infinite. They align every human behavior, to the smallest detail, for unity with God and God's purposes—and nothing else.

The pilgrim band requires a mentor. However, because no single individual can ever achieve the perfection of being mentor to the diversity of people at all the stages of their growth, it is better to say that a pilgrim band requires a mentoring network. It requires a mentor who can surrender that role to another mentor, who in turn can surrender that role to another mentor. Such humility is in fact the mark of a true mentor. A mentor most perfectly represents the *absence of control* over those whom they guide. They can coach, guide, counsel, and advise with courage (for life-on-the-edge) and with wisdom (for life-in-between), and can have the serenity to relinquish their influence to others in a larger process of growth (life-at-peace). They may be gentle or aggressive, accepting or challenging; but in the end, they let go.

The mentoring role is to grow disciples to become mentors in their own right. Each member of the pilgrim band has a destiny and purpose to help others grow in their own journeys. If the disciple fails or resists the emerging role of mentor, it is a sign of moving away from unity with God rather than toward unity with God. The paradox of mentoring is that the more one *desires* and *strives* for unity with God and does not compassionately help others in their spiritual journey, then the more one fails to experience that eternal now when the infinite and finite intersect. And yet the more one *surrenders* desire and *ceases* to strive for self, investing in the growth of others, the more one succeeds in living into that intersection of the infinite and the finite. "Those who want to save their life will lose it, and those who lose their life for my sake, and for the sake of the gospel, will save it" (Mk. 9:35).

An Ordered Life for Cooperation

Spiritual growth requires a new orderliness or intentionality about lifestyle and mission. Lifestyle and personal mission are not separate or compartmentalized aspects of life, in which we invest so much time in one or the other, or devote a tithe to the one and the rest of our financial strength in the other. There must be a seamless unity of lifestyle and mission if we are to pursue life in the spirit. The combination of personal meditation, participation in a pilgrim band, and relationship with a mentor now requires "orderliness" to daily living.

The ancients might have called this a "rule," in which covenanted participants planned their time around work, worship, meditation, learning, and outreach. Physical labor merges with spiritual life to become an act of worship and an aspect of meditation; learning and outreach merge into a single action/reflection experience of growth; the spiritual health of the individual and the global well-being of the community merge into a single mission. The ancient "rule" included specific behavior instructions or limitations that ordered life in the spirit such as the following:

- Moderation: Balance in all things
- Cooperation: Harmony in all actions
- Poverty: Freedom from all obsessions
- Chastity: Purity in all thoughts
- Fidelity: Loyalty to ultimate concern

At first, it might seem that the only way to accomplish such ordered focus on life in the spirit is to retreat to a monastery. Yet even monks have discovered that this can only be one tactic among many. We are discovering new ways to order life in the spirit and merge lifestyle and mission, whether we are on crusade, reforming nations, founding hospitals, starting universities, or even working in business.

A Missional Purpose for a Strangers Salvation

Life in the spirit aligns the individual with a higher purpose in which the individual has a place. The intersection of the infinite and the finite is purposeful. The infinite *yearns* to fulfill itself through the finite, and the finite *yearns* to fulfill itself in the infinite, so that there is one unity of order, meaning, and significance. My mentor spoke of the resolution of "autonomy" (self-centered actualization) and "heteronomy" (controlling structures) in a larger "theonomy" of truth, justice, and love.[2] The meditation focus (the contemporary prayer beads) draws the individual to reflect on four aspects of mission:

- *God's mission:* The redemption, reconciliation, or reunion of the finite and infinite

- *The church's mission:* The multiplication of disciples who experience Jesus the Christ

- *Your group mission:* The particular contribution of your pilgrim band to God's mission

- *Your mission:* The particular use of the conditions of your life to deliver God's mission

The challenge to life in the spirit is rigorous alignment. Individuals and institutions are always being sidetracked away from God's mission to other concerns. They are always being tempted to elevate relative concerns (even very philanthropic and noble concerns) to have *ultimate* importance. Life in the spirit demands rigorous alignment to *ultimate concern*–namely, the overcoming of existential alienation from the infinite and the reconciliation or reunion of the finite. *That* is the concern. Many roads may lead us there, but innumerable temptations also sidetrack us on the way.

It is crucial to life in the spirit that missional purpose connects with compassion for *the stranger*. Traditional processes of outreach or philanthropy carry the hidden assumption that generosity starts "at home," spreads outward to neighbors and acquaintances, and eventually touches faceless and nameless people. To be compassionate, we first must raise our consciousness, understand others, learn their names, and, in a sense, draw them into our circle of acquaintance and friendship. Their inclusion into our inner circle becomes the tacit condition for receiving our generosity.

Life in the spirit contradicts this hidden assumption. One does not need to learn a stranger's name to show compassion to the stranger. The friendship does not come before, but after the act of generosity. That is why such compassion is a great risk, because by not knowing the stranger at all we cannot predict the stranger's reaction. We remain vulnerable in the act of generosity. We are not generous because we have included the other into our circle, but we risk entering *the stranger's* circle to be generous.

The journaling process shared by the pilgrim band, and guided by the mentor, deliberately focuses personal mission in practical ways:

- *This is my life*: Your current experience with Jesus on the road to mission
- *This is our mission*: The compelling, urgent purpose of your pilgrim band or team
- *These are the people*: The current situation of the microculture for whom your heart bursts
- *These are the tactics*: The key strategies to help *that group* experience Christ
- *This is the risk*: The price you are willing to pay to be at the point of mission

This is a strategy to measure the cost of discipleship. The goal is not simply to experience the intersection of the infinite and the finite, but to draw others into that experience as well. To do that, life in the spirit demands that the individual clearly identify what he or she will "stake" in regard to stability, security, comfort, or identity.

The Ultimate Hope for Creation's Final Destination

Life in the spirit is fundamentally about hope. Love, harmony, and joy (as we commonly understand them in organizational life) are mere by-products of that camaraderie shaped around hope. The pursuit of that hope might well lead to offense, conflict, and pain. If the fear of these things causes one to abandon life in the spirit, then hope is lost. This single fact explains the demise of established Christian churches in Western culture today. Fearful of losing autonomy or of confronting heteronomy, they lose the capacity to experience theonomy. Or, to say this less abstractly, established churches fear losing love, harmony, and joy. The more they protect, defend, and guard their churches, the more they lose love, harmony, and joy. Life in the spirit is really about hope— hope for the overcoming of alienation and for the reunion of the infinite and the finite.

I tend to speak of this hope as the reunion of God and humanity, because only humans have been able to elevate the mere chronology of time to the awareness of actual existence. This hope, however, embraces more than humanity. It embraces what we call "the creation," or the world itself and all that is in it. Life-at-peace is experienced occasionally now, but perfectly later, which is only possible if chronology itself is eliminated through the complete intersection of the infinite and the finite. Humanity cannot "exist" without the "context" in which humans live, and humanity cannot be redeemed unless the "context" in which humans live is also redeemed. Life in the spirit anticipates what classical philosophers understood as a reunion of form and essence. Approximations of reality disappear in the "real thing," and intimations of eternity disappear in eternity itself.

ECHO'S JOURNAL _

Life in the spirit! We sat together over an extended lunch in an ordinary restaurant as the mentor explained the simplicity of the spiritual life. We were enthralled.

I see, now, that the mentor has been shaping our receptivity to this all along. Already the rudiments of focused meditation, mentoring relationships, supportive companionships, self-discipline, and unity with creation have been forming in our minds. I am not sure that these disciples, gathered around this table, are my future pilgrim companions. But I am now convinced they are out there. The pilgrim band is a real possibility, and the goal of unity with the infinite through the experience of Jesus the Christ is an authentic quest.

My great-grandparents wanted a job; my grandparents wanted a career; my parents wanted a disposable income; but I want a spiritual life. All the rest can be part of that, but the spiritual life is larger than all the rest.

Yet two things worry me. I am better able to find my position on the talisman map, and I can imagine joining the companions and designing the tactics to fulfill our purpose. Yet the purpose escapes me still. What is our mission? What is my mission? What is the great purpose or calling that would fulfill my life? What exactly do I have, and what exactly should I be doing, daringly and consistently, that will bless a stranger's living?

A second thing troubles me. How do I measure the risks? How do I warn my parents, siblings, and significant intimate other? And my boss, work colleagues, and good buddies? How do I warn all these people so close to me that I am changed and changing, that I have aimed and am aiming at something different?

In my renewed reading about ancient and medieval spirituality (escaping as I am from the entrapments of modernity), I came across the following advice for pilgrims:

> He that be a pilgrim oweth first to pay his debts,
> afterwards set his house in governance
> And then to array himself...
> take leave of his neighbors...
> and simply go forth. (Richard Alkerton, 1406)[3]

I wonder how hard it will be to "simply go forth"?

TENTH MENTORING MOMENT

Where Am I?

The talisman has six existential points, and six experiences of Jesus the Christ. At any given time, each individual may be at any given place on the map. He or she may be immersed in one aspect of existence and far removed from another. She or he may be close to one experience of Jesus the Christ and very distant from another. Knowing where you are gives you clues about where you need to go or what you can anticipate. Sharing your journey with a pilgrim band, and under the guidance of a mentor, can give you help to address your fears, risk strategic moves, and align yourself with God's mission.

Life-on-the-Edge

"Life-on-the-edge" is the attitude of courage that confronts the anxiety of fate and death. It is the assertion of self that makes decisions, causes change, and asserts control. It attempts to make "something" out of "nothing," discern purpose out of futility, and bring order to chaos.

Life-on-the-edge is the *opposition* of two of the points on the diagram. Life is experienced as "edgy," stressful, on the brink of some unknown change, or breaking through to a new state of being. By reflecting on this opposition, one can make better sense of one's current situation and take courage by seeing the potential steps to resolve the stress.

Infinite Beginnings and Intimate Beginnings

The most obvious opposition is between finite beginnings and intimate beginnings. Kairos usurps control from us, transforming our initiatives

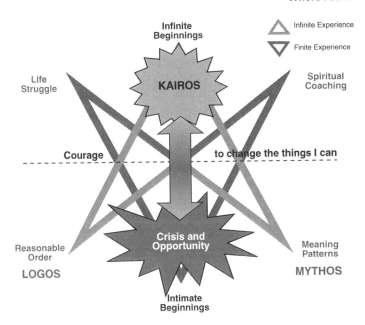

and carrying us away in new relationships and directions. Kairos shatters our anticipations and assumptions, sabotages our best laid strategic plans.

On the other hand, intimate beginnings create opportunities for Kairos to occur. Every crisis is an opportunity; every opportunity is a crisis. Courage lies in the ability to risk a crisis and seize an opportunity. Every victim is a potential entrepreneur.

Life-on-the-edge is lived in the tension between the Cosmic Christ and the Promise Keeper. Every apocalypse carries its own promise; every promise eventually reshapes our lives. If you are most experiencing the Cosmic Christ, look for the Promise Keeper to show you the way. If you are closest to the Promise Keeper, look for the apocalyptic one to both fulfill and transform your expectations. Your next steps look to the right and left. Spiritual coaching and the emergence of meaning patterns discern purpose in the crisis; reason and experimentation bring structure to chaos.

Wally S., the engineer, thought he was prepared for the birth of his first child. He expected it to be as stressful as other beginnings in his life: graduation, marriage, new job, relocation, and so forth. Their pregnancy was a surprise, not part of the strategic plan. He did not know if he really wanted a baby at this time. He was unsure how it would impact his marriage, his financial plan, and his golf game. Still, he figured that between them they would muddle through somehow. When the birth finally happened and his wife died delivering the baby, he was emotionally shattered. He couldn't decide whether to thank God or curse God. He used paternity leave to make arrangements just to survive day to day. Now he is in therapy. He is frightened each day about the absolute uncertainty of the next.

Life Struggle and Patterns of Meaning

Life-on-the-edge also means living in the tension between life struggle and emerging patterns of meaning. The circumstances and limitations that determine our lives challenge preconceived notions, habitual behavior patterns, and community relationships. Suffering breaks complacency, causes us to question assumptions, and pushes us to the brink of despair. We are forced to reinvent ourselves, creating new ways to organize our lifestyles and build credibility for our decisions. We create new patterns of meaning and invest life struggle with new purpose and significance.

Just as life struggle shatters our myths, so also do our patterns of meaning interpret, reshape, and help us overcome life struggle. They bring healing to our brokenness and hope to our despair. "Truth" lies both in the facts and in our interpretation of the facts. Courage is required both in the acceptance of "the facts" and in staking our survival on a particular interpretation of those facts. Reality can render our myths nonsense, and we must have the courage to make sense of the nonsense.

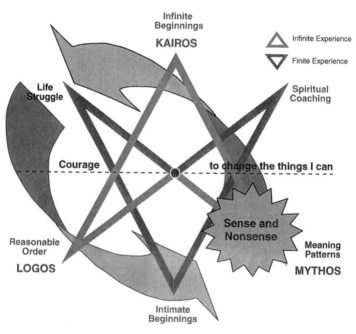

Life-on-the-edge is lived in the tension between the experience of Christ the Vindicator and the experience of Jesus the Healer. The one anticipates or points toward the other. Justice will precipitate healing, and healing will demand justice.

When Mythos is challenged, move to the left or right for next steps. Make nonsense of your myths through reason and relationships to maintain honesty and integrity. Make sense of your struggles through spiritual coaching and openness to the infinite to discern purpose and build or refresh pattern of meaning.

> Antonia, the criminal lawyer, has toiled for years as an assistant district attorney and state prosecutor. She thought she had seen it all—and had become immune to it all. It was only when she began to prosecute cases of child abuse that her courage was put to the test. The evil that she saw drove her to a veritable crusade against injustice to children. And it was a "crusade"—a holy war. Her experiences of Christ the Vindicator, and to a lesser extent Christ as Healer, filled her heart and mind. She had no patience for the church and no mercy on its clergy. Yet the rising tide of child abuse seemed to defeat her crusade, leading her to despair, forcing her to make some sense of the gratuitous evil around her.

Reasonable Order and Spiritual Coaching

Life-on-the-edge is also lived in the tension between the rigorous logic of reason and the intuition of truth beyond reason. Scientists are speculating about truth beyond verifiability; mystics are grounding truth in the proof of our senses. There is "truth" and "Truth," and it is increasingly difficult to sort one from the other. A fog of unknowing clouds our judgment and dims our hope.

> Debra K., the teacher and principal, dedicated her life to the pursuit of truth—and the education of youth to discern the truth. When she accepted the job as assistant principal in an urban core high school, she wanted to raise the standard of academic excellence and overcome social barriers that limited the potential of her students. She had the courage to relocate and live in the very neighborhood where she taught. She took the trouble to learn Spanish and Vietnamese. She was unprepared to discover that the deeper challenge to the future of these kids—and their neighborhood—was neither learning standards nor social injustices. They began turning to her as a mentor to guide them

through ethical ambiguities, discover purpose and meaning, and find hope. She had never thought much about God. Now, from the depths of the urban core and from the questions of her own students, she can think of nothing else.

You must have courage to subject intuition to reason. You must also have courage to surrender reason to intuition. The former courage starts with linear thinking and symbols; the latter courage starts with lateral thinking and portals. Christ may be experienced as the Perfect Human whose mind and behavior mirrors the structure and integrity of the universe, or as the Spiritual Guide whose prophecy and wisdom goes against logic and leads to miracles.

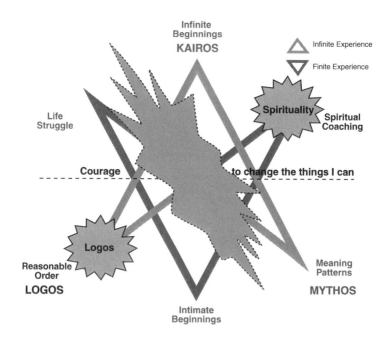

In such a cloud of unknowing, travel from reason to intuition and back again is easily diverted in odd ways. One might veer toward new mythologies to explain the unexplainable and give birth to new relationships. Or one might veer toward supranatural relationships that turn reasonable living upside down.

Life-on-the-edge is a mode of living that all of us experience—not just entrepreneurs, innovators, investigators, and explorers. The age of rationalism has seen the rise of psychotherapy and the proliferation of religions just as the age of superstition saw the rise of science and academic investigation. Life-on-the-edge elevates autonomy. One feels the power to control events and extend one's influence to shape the world. Life-on-the-edge has a mystique of glory that can be very tempting. The exhilaration, however, can quickly turn to exhaustion. Creativity and innovation will reach new heights and depths, but only to be replaced by more creativity and innovation until, in the end, life-on-the-edge is more a pattern of destruction. Unless life-on-the-edge is balanced by life-in-between, life is all rehearsal and no performance. Unless it leads to life-at-peace, it is all fanfare and no finale.

Life-in-Between

"Life-in-between" is the attitude of courage that confronts the anxiety of emptiness and meaninglessness. It is the compromise of self that risks participation in relationships and life. It seeks wisdom to resolve the conflict between logic and faith, make sense of the irrational, and see the truth behind alternative interpretations.

Life-in-between balances the autonomy of life-on-the-edge with limitations that are beyond our control. My mentor described this as the experience of "heteronomy."[1] Life-in-between is precipitated by the finite reaching up to the infinite, and by the infinite interrupting or intruding upon the finite. Therefore, the actual *experience* of intimacy, life struggle, and spiritual coaching is filled with ambiguity and uncertainty. Psychologically, we "feel" caught in between different points of view. Historically, we doubt the outcome of any particular decision. Ethically, we question the moral justification of one option over another. Existentially, we experience anxiety whether we are moving toward acceptance or toward alienation.

Life-in-between is the *juxtaposition* of two infinite points of reference against the middle ground of life experience. Finite living is experienced as torn between two opposing infinite demands. They impose limitations upon our autonomy. They restrict our choices, cause us to hesitate, break our self-confidence, and confuse our strategic plans. The resolution of this ambiguity lies neither to the right nor to the left, but from the experience of Christ that is *across* the diagram.

Between Logos and Mythos

Change always starts with the birth of a relationship and never with the birth of a project. Projects, programs, careers, and even ideas always emerge from the intimate, and often unpredictable, interaction of people.

Intimate beginnings are torn between Mythos and Logos, much like the destiny of a new baby is caught between genetic programming and cultural upbringing. When personality type and skill acquisition alone define selfhood, maturity seems out of reach. Sexuality itself is ambiguously experienced as a combination of physical urge and conditioned consciousness. The birth of anything (person, idea, career, etc.) carries with it an uncertainty beyond our control.

Christ as Vindicator and Christ as Perfect Human will dominate our experience of the infinite, but the hope for a resolution beyond our anxiety lies across the chart.

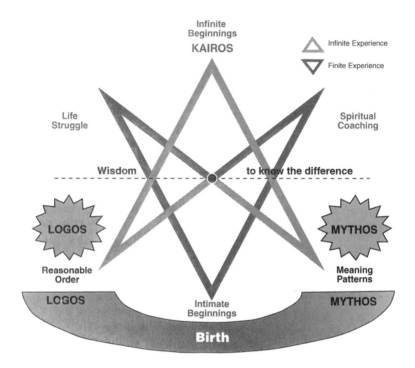

It is the Cosmic Christ, the apocalyptic one, who definitively clarifies our ambiguity. Our hope lies in the Kairos moment, when infinite beginnings clarify and focus the significance of our intimate beginnings and free us for action. Yet as we wait, we look both to Logos and Mythos to understand and discover meaning, however tentative, to our existence.

Wisdom is the ability to know when to accept the limitations imposed on our existence and when to attempt to break out of those limitations. It is the ability to discern between Logos and Mythos, avoiding dogmatism on the one hand and rationalism on the other. The power of the Cosmic Christ to break into existence and birth something new is itself diffused or limited by how we understand, interpret, and apply it to daily living. Our wisdom may stand under the judgment of divine Wisdom, but it is the only means to by which we can grasp and communicate infinite significance.

Bill J., business CEO, is a good businessman and a moral person. He is fair in his dealings, respected by his employees, and loyal to his wife and family. That is, until now. He is not sure how the affair happened. It seemed like he awoke one day, in another bed, and discovered he was in love with another woman. In retrospect, he realized that for some time his affection for a colleague had been growing and that his estrangement from his wife had been deepening. They had had quarrels, of course, but he had not realized how their paths were diverging—and how his path with the "other woman" was converging. Now he is in a divorce proceeding, an acrimonious debate over child custody, and a painful division of property. Is he a bad person? Is he making right choices? Does any of this make sense? Is there any way to reconcile his marriage vows? Can he ever go back to church? Does he ever even want to go back to church? What action will be healthiest for himself, his children, the wife he is leaving, and the woman he thinks he loves?

Between Kairos and Logos

Life-in-between is also experienced in the midst of life struggle. Life would not actually be a struggle if the finite were not yearning to reach

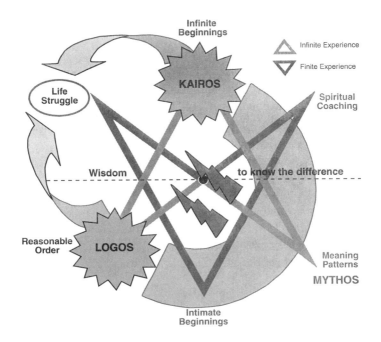

up to the infinite and straining for higher significance. Nor would life be a struggle if we did not sense the infinite reaching down into our life experience, troubling the waters of our soul, and filling us with imaginings beyond our place. Life could easily be mere "chronology," and the only struggle a survival of the fittest. Yet it is not. We are conscious of our *existence,* and we struggle for something more.

Life *is* a struggle because Logos and Kairos are not synchronous under the conditions of existence. Infinite beginnings disrupt reasonable order; and reasonable order limits, directs, and eventually assimilates any new beginning.

In the midst of life struggle, we will sense the Cosmic Christ making radical claims for sacrificial living and Christ the Perfect Human making radical promises for self-fulfillment. Yet the resolution of our struggle lies across the chart, as the Vindicating Christ magnetically draws us from struggle to the discernment of new patterns of meaning, purpose, and destiny.

The renewal of old mythologies or the discernment of new mythologies makes life struggle endurable and reconciles reason with our experiences of gratuitous evil and unexplainable grace.

Wisdom is the ability to persist, persevere, and survive. It is the ability to make sense of irrational evil without surrendering to despair and to interpret miraculous grace without surrendering to fantasy. The power of the Healing Christ is diffused and limited as we develop symbol systems and rationalizations around it. We develop philosophies, religious symbols, liturgies, self-understandings, and worldviews to cope with the struggles of life and to honor both reason and grace.

> Calvin H., the social worker, has worked for non-profit organizations all his life. His particular passion has been the fight against racism. He has marched in protests, lobbied for federal and state legislation, protected illegal immigrants, and generally put his life, lifestyle, and personal security on the line. At the age of fifty-two, he wonders why nothing has changed. He has begun to speculate that there is a deeper reason for racism—and for the persistence of evil and the intransigence of people. He senses that he can no longer be content with transforming society. He needs to transform people—one heart at a time. He's considering doing the one thing he least imagined he might do thirty years ago. He is thinking about training for the priesthood.

Between Mythos and Kairos

Finally, life-in-between is experienced as the ambiguity of spiritual coaching. Is the advice and counsel we receive good or not? Is it helpful or healthy or not? Are the myths with which every person surrounds his or her life "true" or "false"? Is the Kairos we are experiencing divine or demonic? Will it lead to life or death? It is this mentoring that was most prized by the disciples as they sat at the feet of Jesus, the Spiritual Guide. We search for such a mentor—but always live in anxiety about the soundness of the mentor's advice, or when, where, and how that advice should be applied.

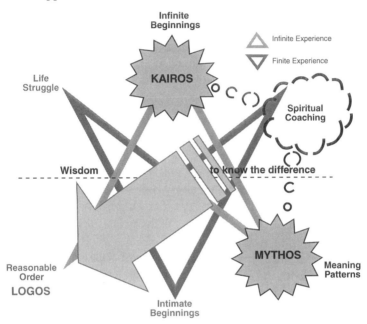

Spiritual coaching is torn between repeating the practices of tradition and openness to apocalyptic change that renders human constructions and symbol systems meaningless. Yet how does the spiritual coach separate ego and prophetic insight?

Christ as a perfect Spiritual Guide had no ego to protect, but even the best spiritual guide can only offer advice under the conditions of his or her existence. The only way to resolve ambiguity and make courageous choices will be to refer to reason—and to Christ the Perfect Human.

Wisdom lies in the ability to evaluate advice and counsel, choose one's own path, and learn from mistakes. It is the ability not only to listen to others but also to think for oneself. The mentoring of Christ the Spiritual Guide is mediated through our own intuitions of the infinite and the credible authorities that interpret patterns of meaning. Life-in-between forces us to discern the difference between authentic faith and mindless cult. Martyrdom is the ultimate test. Will your death be a denial of the truth—or a fulfillment of your life?

Maria S., the surgeon, witnessed a miracle. She doesn't really want to admit that and won't talk to her medical colleagues about it, but it is the only explanation. She assisted in a heart bypass surgery, and the day afterward they lost the patient. The family was gathered around the bed of their mother, and she died. The monitors were "flat lined." The patient had no vital signs at all. In tears, but also in healthy acceptance, the family had joined hands to recite the Lord's Prayer as a final good-bye. At the end of the prayer, the patient started breathing again normally, and vital signs reappeared. Several days later, and far earlier than any recovering patient should, the mother who "was-dead and is alive again" went home. Most of Maria's colleagues would shrug their shoulders and move on, but Maria could not leave it alone. She investigated prayer, interviewed spiritual leaders, and got involved in every religion or cult she could imagine. In the end, she had to bring reasonable order to her work.

Life-in-between encourages a cynicism that can be very tempting. Self-conscious survival, however, always borders on despair and suicide. There can be complacency in constant complaining. The absolute demand to make a commitment beyond oneself can constantly be avoided, and the failure of respite and resolution can always be blamed on someone else or on some situation beyond one's control. Unless life-in-between is balanced by life-on-the-edge, life is all about pendulum swings and class-consciousness and unfair treatment, with no real alternatives.

Life-at-Peace

"Life-at-peace" is the attitude of courage that confronts the anxiety of guilt and condemnation. It is the acceptance of forgiveness, the surrender of self, and reconciliation with the infinite. It experiences serenity in the unity of intimate and infinite beginnings, order and yearning, leadership and fulfillment.

Life-at-peace is the serenity to accept what cannot be changed. If life were only on-the-edge and in-between, lived in the existential tensions of courage and wisdom, it could have only one final outcome: *frustration!* No matter how courageous you were, death would still be inevitable. No matter how wise you were, failure would still be inevitable. Life-at-peace is the absence of ego: striving, yearning, searching, straining, competing, risking, and experimenting. It is also the absence of ambiguity: restrictions, obligations, structures, dilemmas, fears, anxieties, and doubts. It is a resolution and rest, born of compassion and conviction.

The greatest obstacle to serenity is the fundamental inability to accept acceptance. From the autonomous perspective of life-on-the-edge, the experience of ultimate acceptance is offensive. Acceptance is something earned, deserved, or accomplished. That it should simply be received in spite of our effort is unthinkable. Yet that is the radical acceptance of life-at-peace. Our effort may not achieve peace, but God's initiative can bring peace.

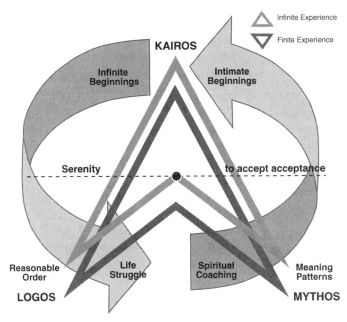

From the heteronymous perspective of life-in-between, the experience of ultimate acceptance is scandalous. Acceptance is something understood, acquired, or learned. That it should simply be received in spite of our wisdom or foolishness is unthinkable. Yet that, too, is the radical acceptance of life-at-peace. Our wisdom may not achieve peace, but God's wisdom can bring peace.

Serenity lies in accepting our acceptance. This is illustrated by a quarter turn of the talisman image. Life is an unbroken continuity, at once comforting and reasonable. God infuses life, and life leads directly to God. All evil can be explained, and everything good can be understood. Life may be challenging, but it is manageable.

The eternal now has been expanded beyond a point in time to time itself. Time stands still. Worship is life itself, and life itself is a single, enduring act of worship. The finite and the infinite are reunited.

Acceptance of things one cannot change is not resignation. It is fulfillment. One's life is caught up in God's life. It is God's doing, marvelous in our eyes.

This "quarter turn" of the talisman is what transforms existence from a state of yearning to a state of acceptance.

- *Struggle is resolved in Logos.* Life makes sense. The structure of the universe and the logic of the mind merge into a single consciousness. You finally say, "I get it now!" The truth and the Truth become one.

- *The quest for mentors is resolved in Mythos.* Life has purpose. Everyone can be a mentor to everyone else, and the patterns of meaning merge into a single celebration. You finally say, "I see it now!" Happiness and Joy become one.

- *Intimate beginnings are resolved in Kairos.* Life has harmony. The ordinary becomes the extraordinary, secular time becomes sacred time, and the profane becomes the sacramental. You finally say, "I'm part of it now!" Relationship and Belonging become one.

Truth and the interpretation of truth are constant. Authenticity and authority become one. Fate is overcome by providence. Life not only is worth living, but it deserves to be preserved. In life-at-peace, the six experiences of Jesus the Christ merge and, in a sense, disappear. The necessity for "incarnation" vanishes because, in the words of Revelation: "God is fully with the people" (see Rev. 21:3).

Maria, Bill, Debra, Wally, Antonia, and Calvin have all exercised courage and wisdom in the tensions of existence. In their own ways they have experienced Jesus the Christ: as healer, guide, vindicator, promise keeper, model for true humanity, or cosmic intruder. Despite their courage and wisdom, life has been frustrating. Certainly they have had successes. Maria has healed people; Debra has guided youth to a better life; Calvin has rescued people from injustice; Bill has nurtured his children; Wally has coped with birth and death; and Antonia has saved many children. Yet their success has been relative at best. Why do they keep going? Why do they keep trying?

Their personal missions have been focused and refined through momentary glimpses of peace. Life-at-peace may have lasted only a few moments, or several days, or even weeks and months before it ended to precipitate them once again into the existence that demands courage and wisdom. Yet they have experienced—tasted, sensed, and intuited—the reunion of the finite and the infinite. It has given them hope.

Will it last? Should it last? Life-at-peace encourages a confidence that can be very tempting. Yet confidence easily turns into condescension. United community turns into cultic harmony. Continuity with current ideas and repeatable practices replaces the passion for total personal growth. This is the moment when a talisman itself can be elevated to the status of ultimate concern—and the moment when either Kairos will shatter complacency with infinite beginnings or human creativity will shatter harmony with intimate beginnings. Unless life-at-peace leads to life-in-between or life-on-the-edge, purposefulness is lost.

These moments of life-at-peace are welcome precisely because they are temporary. They are glimpses of what might be, but which is not yet. The peace that such moments engender can and should change into an even deeper restlessness for the infinite. They propel us forward and cast us once again into life struggle, intimate beginnings, and the quest for spiritual guidance. This is the source of mission. It is this glimpse of the reunion of the finite and the infinite that motivates us to focus our calling, discern our mission, and use our courage and wisdom for the sake of this larger goal that is beyond ourselves.

ECHO'S JOURNAL –

I have been brooding about life—and realize that this is the most mocked activity of modern times. Once observed, the number of ways in which society has discouraged me from brooding about life boggles the mind. I am to be productive, cooperative, and entertained—so that I can be successful, well-liked, and happy. Brooding about life is as unfashionable today as it was when Socrates drank poison and when Jesus was crucified. No more. I refuse to be sidetracked, ending my life in some nursing home asleep before the television screen or complaining that my family doesn't visit me enough.

I've found a pattern to my life-on-the-edge. I am most "on-the-edge" in times of exhilaration, illumination, frustration, anticipation, creativity, righteous wrath, and self-surrender. These are the sensations I experience when I am taking risks, exploring new territory, and growing in unexpected ways. The problem is that each of these experiences so easily crosses an unseen line to become pride, lust, envy, gluttony, covetousness, anger, and sloth. When, exactly, does a lively virtue become a deadly sin?

Much of my life is "in-between," and I half believe that this is exactly where the world wants me. The world wants me to be perpetually "in-between":

always struggling and never winning, always asking questions and never finding answers, always journeying and never arriving. It certainly keeps the fast-food industry going. I think the world is as hostile to life-on-the-edge as it is to life-at-peace. "Not too much exhilaration, please! Don't get fanatical or anything!" "You there! Go easy on the serenity! The nations might disarm, and then where will the economy be?!"

I am beginning to learn how to see things with the peripheral vision of the soul. If you look right at stuff, the way analytical science insists on doing, you tend to miss what is really important. What is important is not what is happening before your eyes, but what is happening just at the edge or horizon of your vision. You can catch a little Kairos out of the corner of your eye. You can see the comforting inevitability of Logos just beyond the confusing complexity of all the collateral damage. I am discovering that you can stare at reality all you want, but a subtle movement, a quiet sound, or a wisp of a fragrance can transport you to a Mythos that is more real than what meets the eye.

Life-at-peace is an enticingly dangerous notion. I have to say that I have experienced peace—true serenity—very seldom in my life, and only very fleetingly. But like a powerful drug, it leaves you straining for more. Therein lies the danger. Peace is not something "achievable," but only "receivable." It is attainable only because the infinite is not indifferent to the finite, as the mentor once said.

What would it be like to stay to experience, and remain within, the eternal now? How would it feel if intimate beginning had an equal, and proportionate, infinite import? If every infinite beginning led to a commensurate deepening of intimacy? What if for every struggle you had a spiritual guide? And for every question you received a clear and sensible reply? Order would overcome struggle, and meaning would require no cultural forms to be fully understood. What would it be like, not just to understand but to be understood? What would it be like, not only to be accepted by the infinite but to accept that acceptance? I guess that would be heaven.

PART 2

Talisman Practice

*An Alternative
Spiritual Discipline*

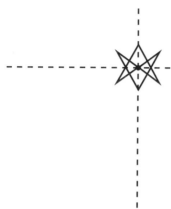

The Ancient Rosary

These past weeks we have been introduced to a most intriguing spiritual discipline. It is aimed at omniliterate people like me—people who actually read very little but learn mostly through images, sounds, videos, films, and symbol systems. My great-grandparents were Builders and read books; my Boomer grandparents read magazines; my Buster parents read e-mail and surfed the Internet; I multitask all of the above, all at once, and tie it altogether with a tattoo, a logo, or a symbol. I never understood why until the mentor explained it to me. It's all about talismans: images that are portals to the infinite, objects that connect the soul as well as the mind to greater meaning.

This alternative discipline struck me at first as rather bizarre—even medieval. I had always thought of a rosary as, I don't know, some kind of silly magic for the unenlightened. But the more I thought about it, the more I saw images and objects used by quite intelligent people. Buddhists use prayer beads and meditation devices; so also do Native Indians, Hindus, Jews, Muslims, and on and on. It seems that nobody relies on mere words and the sheer abstractions of the mind except modern-day North American Christians. Perhaps John Dewey and the public school system have done us a disservice? Gosh, isn't that hard to imagine! Maybe we are missing something?

The truth is that my life is filled with talismans, shallow or profound, for better or worse. My clothing, adornments, computer screen savers, cell phone rings, dangling objects on my rearview mirror, pictures in my office, and the interior decoration of my home are all talismans. People on my street are landscaping their yards and shaping their shrubs in images of the infinite.

Yet I still find prayer beads to be a bit weird. It makes me think teenagers are about to take up knitting (which, I am told, is a new trend). It makes me think religious book stores are going to earn more income from selling dream-catchers, window hangings, bookmarks, videos, and t-shirts than they earn selling actual books (which, I am told, is also the new trend). Among other things from which I am lapsed, I am a lapsed Catholic. I always thought the rosary was all about the Virgin Mary. I'm basically interested in God. Prayer beads are a method to connect with God—perhaps we need saints and mentors and objects and disciplines to point the way.

I think the thing that bothers me most about using prayer beads is that you have to train for it. You have to work at it. You have to keep doing it until it becomes as familiar as breathing. I'm used to instant gratification. I treat my relationship with God like most of my other intimate relationships—it's supposed to just happen, and I shouldn't have to work at it. Given the track record of love and marriage among my peers, perhaps I am wrong about that, too.

Well, after all, prayer beads are more relevant and helpful than I had thought. They are portable, profound, and great conversation starters. Most of all, the prayer beads keep me focused. Two seconds of silence is about all I can handle. Unless I am holding something in my hand, counting out the steps, and concentrating on one image at a time, my mind is apt to wander all over the place.

I heard the mentor speak at a retreat for senior CEOs in business, and this is what he shared…

A Common Devotional Object

The Teaching

The rosary has been a discipline of spiritual life and reflection for centuries. Before the printing press and the ability to make the words of the Bible accessible in all languages and to all literate people, the rosary—along with other devotional objects, icons, and images—was the method through which spiritual life merged with daily lifestyle. It was accessible at any time, in any place, and among any companionship. The touch of it, the ordering of life and memory around the beads, the methodology of prayer all provided solace, instruction, strength, motivation, and serenity in good times and bad.

The advent of the printing press replaced talismans with words in linear form, grammar, abstractions, and concepts. Literacy became a necessary means to spiritual life. Ironically, the very justification by works the Reformation opposed became a de facto requirement for Protestant salvation. Now we had justification *through* literacy. One needed to gain mastery of translation, diction, grammar, punctuation—and ultimately of analysis, abstraction, and concept—to understand, contextualize, apply, and live out the Christian life. Gradually, experience of the Spirit was replaced by understanding of the Spirit. Christians became more a people of "the book" than people of "relationship with Jesus."

As the world became industrialized and then secularized, this same abstraction and analysis became the foundation of scientific methodology. Public literacy became even more important in order for people to study a much more narrowly defined truth. Scientific methodology, analysis, and abstraction became increasingly important to all fields of knowledge—and so also for economic gain, career advancement, and human control over nature and God.

Yet as the twentieth century concluded, disillusionment with scientific methodology and analytical truth grew. Gratuitous evil and radical grace could not be either explained or explained away. The yearning not only for relationship with others but also for relationship with God increased. Science began to explore waves instead of data bytes. The supernatural began to attract renewed attention. Meaning began to surpass language; truth began to escape words. The advent of the computer opened a new world of image, video clip, and sound.

Just as we left the preliterate world for the literate world, so now in the twenty-first century we leave the literate world for the omniliterate world. It is not that we are abandoning analytical truth; we are just going beyond it again. Talisman is once again taking its place alongside word.

Talisman is both symbol and portal. As symbol, it is the object, image, or data byte that reminds one of eternal truths imperfectly expressed in words. Yet even more significantly, as portal, the talisman is the vehicle through which the Holy reaches out to touch our lives. The Holy uses the talisman to heal, reassure, strengthen, encourage, judge, and even transform life. The object of meaning that one holds, sees, touches, embraces, strokes, tastes, hears, and shares—the object of infinite import the mere recognition of which provokes conversations, dialogues, arguments, and spontaneous community—has become a second and perhaps more potent methodology of truth than even science.

Spirituality and faith, too, have been returning to the talisman way of experiencing and reflecting about God. Devotional objects abound; computer-generated images flood our worship; drama replaces liturgies of mere words. Faith development is less about presentation than conversation; less about education than experience. Relationship is more important than membership; how one lives is more important than what one knows. Most important of all, the experience of Jesus is more important than knowledge about Jesus.

Yet in the explosion of individual religion and personally meaningful talismans, is there an opportunity for a common devotional object to once again bond Christian pilgrims together as it did in premodern, medieval, and ancient times? Perhaps the precise rubrics of the rosary are hard to translate into postmodern times, but the principles and the methodology and the purposefulness can be applied. An old instrument can be used in a fresh way to help postmodern pilgrims center their lives and lifestyles around Jesus the Christ.

The Ancient Rosary

The ancient rosary used a necklace of fifty-nine beads strung together in a numerical pattern to guide prayerful Christians to meditate on their experience—their relationship—with Christ. In the brightest day or the darkest night one's fingers could automatically follow a spiritual path, and meditation could alter behavior.

The rosary traditionally celebrates three distinct mysteries of grace related to Christ. One might focus on any given mystery either in response to the Christian year or in response to personal need.

1. The first mystery is the story of the birth of Jesus, beginning with the annunciation, then Elizabeth's words of greeting to Mary, the nativity, the presentation of the infant Jesus in the temple and prophecies of Simeon and Anna, and the discovery of the child Jesus teaching in the temple.

2. The second mystery is the story of the death of Jesus, beginning with his agony in the garden of Gethsemane, then his scourging, crowning with thorns, journey to the cross, and final crucifixion.

3. The third mystery is the story of his glorification, beginning with his resurrection, then his ascension, gift of the Holy Spirit, the assumption of Mary, and her role as intercessor in behalf of humankind.

These three mysteries sound both familiar and foreign to Protestant ears; and yet they connect powerfully with postmodern, pagan people out of their own hopes, struggles, and experiences. One touches—fingers—the rosary with as much hope and comfort as classic Protestants might touch or clasp the Bible. The words are less important than the act itself. The Holy reaches through the portal of the talisman to impact our souls for comfort and challenge.

The pendant part of the necklace provides a foundation or preface to the discipline of prayer and reflection. One begins the discipline by touching the cross, feeling its jagged edges, perhaps feeling the image of Christ crucified and now risen.

- Holding the cross, repeat the Apostles' Creed
- Touching the first bead, recite the Lord's Prayer
- Touching the next three beads, recite the angelic greeting of Mary ("Hail Mary"), a reminder of the saving significance of the incarnation, and also the "Gloria Patri," a part of the common Christian liturgy
- Focusing on the icon joining the pendant to the necklace and carrying the image of both Jesus and Mary, lift up personal supplications or intercessory prayers
- Turning to the five sets of ten beads ("decades"), each set divided by a single bead, one recites the Lord's Prayer, "Hail Mary," or "Gloria Patri" with each set
- Feeling the individual bead dividing the "decades," reflect on whatever event is the focus of the mystery: of Jesus' birth, death, or glorification
- Concluding the cycle, make further prayers of supplication or intercession, followed by the Lord's Prayer and the Apostle's Creed

No doubt one can use the traditional rosary with much more complexity and rigor, but this basic pattern reveals the methodology and meaning behind the talisman. The common use of the rosary binds Christian brothers and sisters together, even when they meet as strangers.

The rosary is intended for use both as a group and as an individual exercise. The congregation, monastic community, or pilgrim may use a talisman in corporate worship, praying and reciting aloud and in unison. Alternatively, the rosary is intended for use by an individual for private devotion, as a regular spiritual discipline, or as an intervention in times of peril or anxiety.

However the rosary is used, the discipline does not stand alone, but should involve the individual in a larger lifestyle of grace and service. The discipline of the rosary should

- draw the disciple into sincere self-analysis, confession, and repentance
- involve the disciple in the sacramental experience of Christ found in authentic Christian community and in the Eucharist
- compel the disciple to participate in Christian mission through deeds of compassion and justice

This ability of the talisman to link seeker or disciple with a lifestyle of sincerity and integrity, intimate healthy relationships, and sacrificial giving is particularly appealing to postmodern people. Any discipline involving devotional objects can be reduced to perfunctory actions or magical manipulation. This temptation is true for those who use the rosary, or for those who use the printed words and bound books of the Bible, or for those who use any image or object as a focus for meditation. Given the selfish nature of humanity, it is always possible (perhaps even probable?) that an object (necklace or book, litany or memorized verses) can be so elevated to ultimate concern that it replaces the true spiritual target of the devotion. This is why such disciplines are best done in a community, group, or pilgrim band, among those who can challenge and encourage one another to focus on the goal of the discipline rather than the discipline itself.

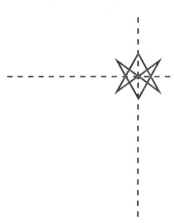

The Hope Rosary

Contemporary Prayer Beads

The motivation to develop an alternative discipline with the rosary comes from the postmodern shift in learning methodology and from the postmodern quest for authentic spiritual experience. Our world has shifted from the rational, abstract linear learning of books and curriculums to the intuitive, relational, and lateral learning of images and storytelling. Literacy is not unimportant, but the postmodern world is recapturing the power of devotional objects, moving pictures, and stories. Similarly, our world has shifted from simple materialism and manipulative pragmatism to an aching search to experience God incarnate in lifestyle. People are not any less selfish or shallow, but material success and scientific progress simply fail to satisfy the itch for God.

The alternative here starts with the conviction that any spiritual discipline that has real value will draw the participant into sincere self-analysis. That analysis will both precipitate and support serious change in life and lifestyle. Our experience with addiction has revealed that to be effective the discipline must involve the participant in a larger, authentic community that is focused on experience and is celebrating a relationship with a "Higher Power"—God incarnate. Finally, the alternative here reflects the ancient convictions that abundant life cannot be experienced until it is given away and that spiritual life is only completed through moral service.

Perhaps the greatest strategic flaw in the traditional use of the rosary is that it assumes background knowledge of the Christian story and a familiarity with liturgical tradition that is simply no longer present in the "post-Christendom" world. Much of the language and terminology of the rosary is no longer intelligible to high-school dropouts or academic specialists, nor is it familiar to career professionals or the average person on the sidewalk or in the shopping mall. A truly helpful spiritual discipline will help you change your life and lifestyle—but it cannot assume that first you must change your lifestyle and language to just begin the spiritual discipline.

What is needed is a way to customize the discipline of the rosary for each individual in the demographic and lifestyle diversity of contemporary culture. One can preserve the principles of the rosary, but reimagine the tactics for its use.

The alternative here preserves both the Christ-centered and incarnational nature of the rosary and the methodology of prayer and reflection. It supports the team-based discipline of small group and corporate worship and the individual discipline that finds strength in the midst of grinding routine or stress. The alternative

- allows the individual to insert those scriptures, liturgies, hymns, stories, images, or other meditative foci from the history of faith and individual life experience that are most relevant, uplifting, and powerful
- uses the six experiences of Jesus the Christ (Cosmic Christ, Vindicating Christ, and Christ the Perfect Human; Jesus the Promise Keeper, Jesus the Healer, and Jesus the Spiritual Guide) in place of the three "mysteries"
- closes the discipline with intentional focus on mission, helping the individual move from confession to thanksgiving to mission—or from self-examination to self-fulfillment to self-surrender

This is why I have given the name "Hope Rosary" to this alternative spiritual discipline. If the traditional rosary draws people to look backward in time from a Christendom perspective, the Hope Rosary encourages people to look forward in time from a pagan context. It is designed less for comfort and more for perseverance. It is intended less for memory and more for action. It is concerned less with where Jesus was and more with where Jesus is going in the future course of salvation history. It attempts to lead the Christian from contemplation into mission that is a fulfillment of oneself and a blessing to humankind.

The Hope Rosary is simply another form of prayer beads, which in turn is another form of talisman. The power for the prayer beads, like the power of any talisman, lies in the experience of both symbol and portal.

As symbol, the power of the prayer beads lies in constant repetition and familiarity. Once the discipline is learned and repeated over and over again, it becomes a spiritual habit that helps the individual concentrate on what really matters. It is portable, profound, and provides a structure for reflection. It focuses the mind on meaning and purpose.

As portal, the power of the prayer beads lies in evocative listening. The beads are a sensory experience that makes the Holy "touchable" and "incarnate." Using the Hope Rosary draws the infinite into contact with the finite; it allows God to be in "conversation" with the individual. Regardless of the words exchanged, one finds a sense of immediacy that offers comfort, strength, clarity, courage, and hope.

There is no one way to use the alternative rosary, because portions of the discipline may be different from person to person or from time to time in any individual experience.

Hold a rosary (what we are calling the Hope Rosary) in your hands so that your left hand contains the beads of the string and your right hand touches the pendant and the cross. Your fingers touch each bead as you pray and meditate, using words from tradional church liturgy, as in the following example (illustrated further in the Appendix on p. 176).

THE CROSS PENDANT—*The Chalcedonian Confession and/or Words of Institution for Holy Communion*

Jesus Christ, fully human, fully divine, infinite paradox, crucial for abundant life.

and/or

Take, eat, this is my body, broken for you. Eat this in remembrance that Christ died for you, and feed on him in your heart with thanksgiving.

THE SINGLE BEAD—*The Apostles' Creed*

I believe in God the Father Almighty, Maker of heaven and earth. And in Jesus Christ, His only Son our Lord, who was conceived by the Holy Spirit, born of the Virgin Mary, suffered under Pontius Pilate, was crucified, died, and was buried. On the third day he rose again from the dead. He ascended into heaven, and sits at the right hand of God the Father Almighty. From thence he shall come to judge the living and the dead. I believe in the Holy Spirit, the holy catholic church, the communion of saints, the forgiveness of sins, the resurrection of the body, and the life everlasting. Amen.

THE NEXT THREE BEADS

1. The Lord's Prayer—Our Father, who art in heaven, hallowed be thy name. Thy kingdom come, thy will be done, on earth, as it is in heaven. Give us this day our daily bread; and forgive us our trespasses, as we forgive those who trespass against us. And lead us not into temptation, but deliver us from evil, for thine is the kingdom, and the power, and the glory, forever. Amen.

2. The Serenity Prayer—God grant me the serenity to accept the things I cannot change; the courage to change the things I can; and the wisdom to know the difference.

3. Personal Intercessory Prayers for Strangers to Grace—(Begin with strangers you have encountered casually or significantly in the past hour, and work outward in time).

THE SINGLE BEAD— *"Fear Not" from Isaiah 41:10*

Fear not, for I am with you. Be not afraid, for I am your God. I will strengthen you; I will help you; I will uphold you with my victorious right hand.

THE ICON WITH THE IMAGE OF CHRIST

• Meditations on your life-on-the-edge
• Meditations on your life-in-between

Note: This can also be a time of dialogue and mutual critique with your colleagues in the "pilgrim band" as you help one another discern your position in life.

DECADES (TEN BEADS, REPEATED FIVE TIMES)

1. Cosmic Christ
2. Vindicating Christ
3. Christ the Perfect Human
4. Jesus the Promise Keeper
5. Jesus the Healer
6. Jesus the Spiritual Guide
7. God's mission: Redemption of the world
8. Church's mission: Multiplication of disciples
9. Your partnership (congregation, organization, pilgrim band) mission
10. Your personal mission

SINGLE BEADS BETWEEN DECADES—*The Lord's Prayer or Serenity Prayer*

Repeat the discipline of each decade, interspersed by prayer, five times around the necklace, until your fingers return to the central icon. One variation is to complete just one decade and return to the central icon.

THE ICON WITH THE IMAGE OF CHRIST

Meditations on your life-at-peace

Trace the discipline back down the pendant of beads in reverse order.

THE SINGLE BEAD —*Isaiah 41:10*

THREE BEADS: THE NEXT THREE BEADS

1. Personal prayers of thanksgiving
2. Serenity Prayer
3. The Lord's Prayer

SINGLE BEAD—*The Creed*

THE CROSS PENDANT—*Chalcedonian Confession or Words of Institution*

Take, eat, this is my blood, shed for you. Drink this in remembrance that Christ died for you, and feed on him in your heart with thanksgiving.

Prayer beads do for the individual what corporate liturgy in worship does for the community. They provide structure or form in order to mediate on the experience of the infinite to the finite. The discipline creates an eternal now, a sacred experience apart from the chaos of common time in which the individual can experience the New Being of Christ and so experience renewed being in their daily lives. What is often mistaken for radical personalization of religion is really an experience of radical community. In the experience of the talisman, individuality itself is surrendered into a larger unity. Just as the individual surrenders self to the mystery of God, so the individual loses self in compassion for the world.

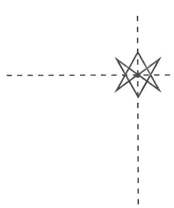

First Dialogue

My encounters with Mentor always elicit the same reaction. He sits in the corner of the café, oddly normal. I'm not sure what I really expect to see. Lord Byron with brooding eyes? A charismatic athlete exuding health? A Hollywood philanthropist complete with book table and videotapes? Instead, he looks like the kind of person no one would be able to describe in a police report. Just a guy—average height, average complexion, going a little bald, dressed in khaki, cell phone on belt, coffee in hand. The only remarkable thing about him is that he communicates a general sense of restlessness. There is a posture about him that suggests we have more to talk about, but our time is about up. He isn't looking over his shoulder or at his watch, but he seems to be expecting something, or someone, to call him away. And he seems to be looking forward to it, but it does not make him view his present company with any disfavor.

The "present company" is a curious mix of generation, gender, culture, and economy. True, the boundary between those who are merely pausing to eavesdrop (waiting for their latte), those who have paused for a while to listen, those who have decided to stay, and those who have been there from the beginning seems rather vague. They all seem to assume equal rights in posing questions and making comments. I myself have come looking for him, told he was here by a colleague at the office. He tends to locate in different places, not with the air of someone eluding pursuit, but with the air of someone pursuing something but glad for company. I wonder how many here and now are like me, starting out as an eavesdropper at the food court, pausing to hear more at the sports arena, and now prepared to hang around a while in the café. In retrospect, the conversation from all these places and times merges together as a single discussion; but I have a memory that certain things were repeated often, that other things were said only once, and that repetition was no sure sign of significance.

Familiar as I am with meetings, lectures, seminars, and PowerPoint presentations at work—and chatter, competition, argument, and four-letter-word posturing in public—dialogue with the mentor is refreshingly respectful and intimidatingly honest. Perhaps it is that alone that arrests attention and draws people into the conversation. There are no rules, but two habits, each reinforced in different ways.

The first habit is that everyone refers to him as "Mentor." It is always "Mentor, tell me this" or "Mentor, why do you say that?" or even "Mentor, I think you're crazy!" It creates the creepy sensation that you are really sitting in the agora at Athens or resting on a pile of stones beside the Sea of Galilee or pausing outside the doors of a monastery. The mentor himself seems to care not at all about the title. This peculiar habit of addressing him seems to be reinforced by the group itself; and no one, not even idle eavesdroppers, seems to object.

The second habit is decidedly unusual, deliberately and aggressively reinforced by the mentor himself. No one is allowed to speak without first stating his or her first name. Of course, if the dialogue is rapid-fire between the mentor and another or between a specific pair of participants, it flows uninterrupted. But if a new person interjects or a participant in the dialogue falls silent and then speaks again, the new person will state his or her name first before making a comment or asking a question. Occasionally, someone will forget, and the mentor will immediately interrupt and ask for the name.

Once in my hearing, a relatively new eavesdropper became angry at this habit and flatly refused to state her name. The mentor (and everybody else, for that matter) just stared at her expectantly until she gave it. If a person refused utterly to give a first name, the mentor would intentionally ignore the comment or question.

"Mentor, why do you insist that every statement or question be prefaced with an introduction of one's name?" someone asked.

"Because no true dialogue can occur in anonymity," the mentor replied unhesitatingly. "And if truth only emerges from dialogue, then anonymity is the enemy of truth. Anonymity is the primary tool of manipulation and deception. Those who refuse to identify themselves in conversation are seeking to remove themselves from accountability in conversation. God knows who they are. Will they deceive God? Their partners in conversation have a right to know who it is that addresses them. It is a moral obligation. In dialogue,

Truth intersects with Existence. The infinite in its unity connects with the finite represented by the diversity of our separate personalities and minds, raising the possibility of insight. No one can hide in personal anonymity without jeopardizing the opportunity of growth for all. Therefore, who are you? What is your name? Are you willing to have a stake in the dialogue or not? If there is no risk, there is no real dialogue. If the dialogue collapses, the infinite recedes; and insight is no longer possible. If insight is no longer possible, we are wasting our time and may as well finish our coffee and leave."

That is how conversations with the mentor are experienced. Whether these conversations are short or long; whether they occur around coffee tables, bar rooms, or huddled in the arena; whether people stay for a while, or hurry to other appointments—all will agree that these conversations are time well spent. We feel fresher, cleaner, clearer, better, and more focused for it. Here I am again. "Mentor, I am Echo. Let me ask why...?"

The Teaching

"Mentor, my name is Maria."

The mentor smiled shyly. "Maria, it looks as if you just stepped out of the surgery to find some stimulating caffeine. You will have to sterilize yourself all over again." Obviously, she was dressed in the white gown doctors wear in hospitals, and rubber gloves peaked out of her pocket.

"Only too true! That is the just the issue. I am a doctor. I deal in life-and-death issues, but I am too busy to think about them. People fall apart all around me, but I must remain calm. I only know two speeds: rush and stop. When I do get a vacation, it takes me three weeks to even try to contemplate a philosophical idea. I gave up church. They were never open when I was available. Besides, they were strategically planning trivialities when I needed help doing triage. What can I do?"

The mentor leaned forward, but another interrupted. "Exactly!" he said. The mentor looked at him intently. "I'm Bill. That's exactly my issue. Maybe I'm not doing open-heart surgery, but I run a large company. I've got R&D, HR, Marketing, and Accounting people demanding my attention all the time—meetings, phone calls—the only reading I do catches me up on the competition. I'm going through my second divorce, and my kids hardly know my name. God could be speaking, but I have my cell phone turned off. How do I tune in?"

The mentor removed a string of beads from his pocket and pulled them through his fingers thoughtfully. He glanced at Maria, Bill, and the others. "You need a diagnostic tool for spiritual health, perhaps. It needs to be portable, simple, and effective. Something you can use on the run, in the rain, and under pressure. Reliable. Like a compass in a jungle. Let me tell you about mine." He paused and looked up suddenly. "My best R&D people reengineered an old technology. Once, they called it a 'rosary.' I call it a 'Hope Rosary.' Touch it." He passed it around.

The looks on the faces of the group ranged from skepticism to hostility. "My great-grandmother carried one of these out of habit from the 'old country,'" one person remarked dubiously. "She was a lovable relic herself."

"Isn't this what people used in the Middle Ages?"

"Yeah. I saw it in a grade B Dracula movie."

"I'll wear it to my next board meeting," scoffed Bill, "and put it down on the table next to my *Blackberry* so I can grab it if God text messages me."

"Feel it," Mentor continued. "The talisman can be any shape or texture. These beads are made of black steel because I prefer them to be cold to the touch. The cold reminds me of death—my death, of course. It is impossible to contemplate life without first facing the inevitability and immanence of one's own death. But perhaps some other shape, texture, material, color, or substance will be a more suitable talisman for you. That is the way of talismans. This talisman will remind you of eternal truth, as I shall demonstrate. But you must also allow the infinite to speak to you, interrupt you, grip you by the throat and shake you perhaps. A true talisman screams into your inner heart: *'Listen! Listen! Pay attention! You are going to die soon! It may be tomorrow or in fifty years, but in the perspective of infinity that is just one molecule away!'"*

A customer hurried by, eyeing us with some anxiety, and exited quickly, slamming the door.

"The talisman is portable. You can touch it on the elevator between meetings, experience it in the park over lunch, and even feel it against your flesh in the midst of other activities. It requires no batteries. It will not rust. It attracts no unwanted attention and demands no setup. Of course, almost anything can become a talisman, but the Hope Rosary is a more complex one. The series of beads and pendants is like Morse code—dots and dashes combined in a meaningful way to telegraph the infinite or to allow the infinite to telepath the finite. My version is rather different from the ancient version, but the principles are the same. It's "church-on-the-move," "sacrament-to-go"—it's a millennial operating system against which you can interface any existential software, a never-ending prayer of the subconscious mind that unites the segments of a fragmented life."

"How do you turn it on?" a member of the group asked. "Sorry. I'm Wally. An engineer. We look for the on/off switch."

Mentor laughed. He took the necklace from Wally. "Hold it in your hands this way," he said. "I am right-handed, so I drape the necklace through my left hand and grasp the cross pendant with the fingers of my right hand. This is what 'turns it on.' Feel the roughness, the sharpness of the crucifix. Stare at the image of pain and death. It is special. Unique. Remember the ancient fifth-century confession: 'Jesus…fully human and fully divine…infinite paradox…crucial for salvation.' Do not try to analyze this. I know, it is hard to do. You are an engineer. Indeed, all of you are modern people. You have been educated in the philosophy of John Dewey, shaped in the formal education system, convinced of scientific method. Nevertheless, do not analyze the talisman. It is a paradox, essentially nonrational, an incarnation, an intersection of the infinite and the finite. Just 'be there' to the infinite, and let the infinite 'be there' to you. This is the essence of incarnation. It just is. You are what you are. God says 'I am who I am.' Stare at each other across the chasm of existence."

An intrusive voice broke the silence. "Grande, low-fat, decaf latte— easy on the foam—extra hot." Nobody heard it.

"For many of us, our last enduring memory of church was our first communion or confirmation. Our only contact with Christendom is Christmas Eve. Hold the cross pendant, and remember the words of institution the priest utters before the sacrament of communion. Repeat them:

"Take, eat, this is my body broken for you. Eat this in rememb-rance that Christ died for you, and feed on him in your heart through faith with thanksgiving."

This is the food. The talisman is the food. You don't have to be at church, and you certainly don't have to quarrel about bread that is cubed, wafered, or broken; or leavened or unleavened; or served standing, sitting, or crawling. It's real, it's available right now, so have some!"

One of us interrupted. "I'm Antonia. Are you saying that this talisman is evidence of an infinite reality beyond our perception? Furthermore, is it your personal testimony that this is a process of incorporating infinite values into daily living?"

"Uh-oh," muttered a younger man in blue jeans. "There's a lawyer in our midst."

Mentor considered the question a moment. "Yes and no. Yes, one result of the discipline of the Hope Rosary is that lifestyle and values will be reshaped through contact with the infinite. However, the talisman does not provide evidence of the infinite. The talisman is a portal through which the infinite is really, truly, fully present in the finite. It is the 'real presence' of God that you experience, just as in the sacrament. It is an incarnation. In a sense you are 'ingesting' God through the Hope Rosary, just as you might partake of bread and wine at the Eucharist. But beware! In another sense God is 'ingesting' you! We leap to think that God is 'really present' to us, but we fail to realize that we become 'really present' to God. This gap, this alienation that we call 'existence,' makes humanity as unreal to the infinite as the infinite seems unreal to us. In the end, salvation and hope itself do not lie in taking a little piece of the infinite into the finite. They lie in the infinite's taking the entirety of our existence into itself. It is our unity with God that is our hope—not a piece of God carried in our pocket."

"What next?" asked Wally, ever practical.

"Move your finger from the cross pendant to the first bead. It is a separate—and individual—bead. Recite the Apostles' Creed aloud or silently. Why that creed? Well, it is an ancient one, and a comprehensive one. There are others, of course. What I like about it, however, is what it does *not* include. Most of the creeds that followed these two most ancient ones (I mean the Chalcedonian Confession and Apostles' Creed) were driven to include theological or ideological nuances in response to the politics of the time. Here you have an ancient purity, an essential faith that predates Christendom itself. It is an ancient consensus and, therefore, has more credibility for postmodern people."

"So do you think it refers to the 'Catholic Church' (with the capital *C*, meaning Papal Rome) or not? I'm Calvin." He was the young man in blue jeans.

"It's a question of inclusivity for you?" Mentor asked. Calvin nodded.

"I mean 'catholic church' in the sense of the universal church—spelling the word with a small *c*. But that is a modern issue, an old issue—and frankly, an irrelevant issue. Do any of you really care about distinctions between Catholic, Protestant, and Orthodox churches? Of course not. The twenty-first–century issue is whether the creed should refer to a catholic *church!* I would prefer the words 'catholic *community*' or even 'catholic *communities.*' Or perhaps we could say 'catholic *networks* or *alliances.*' What we truly believe in is not catholic institutions, properties, hierarchies, liturgies, and the professional clergy who mediate it all; we believe in catholic relationships, attitudes, behavioral habits, and the credible leaders who model it all. The rosary (both the ancient one and the reengineered version) is really a method for ordinary people, in real relationships, to experience God, without institutional regulation or interference. That is the power of talisman. It is not anti-institutional. It is institutionally indifferent."

Calvin replied: "I do recall that some versions of the Apostles' Creed include the words 'he descended into hell'' when talking about Christ. Do you?"

Again, Mentor considered the question, taking a sip of coffee. "Not usually. The touch of the pointed crucifix is reminder enough, and more efficient a portal than the added abstraction of words. Yet it makes sense. The ancient images of the 'harrowing' or 'breaking' of hell are very powerful. Most people think of hell only as a punishment for their enemies or as a threat to keep them honest. They do not expect to *meet Jesus* there. They do not see the implicit liberation and hope in the image. They see only an ugly gate, looming and locked. They do not see the *broken* gate. They do not see the depth of being shattered by the power of being."

Mentor looked about the café, musing aloud and yet to himself. "Existence," he said, "is like a veneer that masks the depth of being. Sometimes we draw it over us; sometimes it overshadows us. It is like the smoked glass of this tabletop. From above you can see nothing through the glass; it is dark, opaque. Only by staring at it for a time do you begin to see through existence the dark underside—the dirt, dried gum. The waitress will clean and sterilize the top, but the bottom festers with germs. See the people here—pleasant, polite, a veneer of cheerful optimism. Yet perhaps that one has cancer, or that one has a son stationed in Iraq, or that one is about to see his divorce lawyer. What if God met them at the gates of hell? So, yes, the metaphor is appropriate, whether or not you say the words."

"What next?"

Mentor turned again to the rosary of beads in his hand. "After the single bead for the Apostles' Creed, you find three beads in a row. These represent the core prayers—the ancient and contemporary prayers—of life. The first is the Lord's Prayer. I think of this prayer more as incantation than theology. Books have been written interpreting the *theology* of the prayer, but to what purpose? The words are plain. The meaning is clear. What we neglect is the power that flows through the words. The words draw us up from the depth of being into the awareness of existence itself. We "surface," so to speak, on the plane of existence, aware that it is existence. To become aware of it is, in a sense, to stand apart from it, vulnerable to the in-break of Kairos. These are not words to *think about*. They are words to savor. Say them, and lick your lips in anticipation."

He continued. "The second core prayer is the *Serenity Prayer*. This is the best-known prayer in the world today. And yes, this prayer does *require thought*. It is deeply introspective, and it poises your imagination to revisit your life as on-the-edge, in-between, and at-peace. We cannot help but ask ourselves: What serenity? What courage? What wisdom? Do I really possess any of those things?

"We use this prayer in my AA meeting." One of the participants had taken advantage of another sip of coffee to interrupt with some frustration. "We do the routine, you know. I say 'Hi, I'm Wally, and I'm an alcoholic,' and everyone replies, 'Hi Wally.' We all pray the prayer from memory; the gavel falls; and we get on with the first-step stuff. After you've done it twenty times, you don't even think about it. It means nothing."

"That is because you do not have a guide or a leader," Mentor replied. "That is the strength and weakness of the twelve-step program. It places everyone on the same level. You feel the power of belonging and shared struggle, but without a mentor you simply pool ignorance and share tears. The pilgrim band is different. We have a leader and, therefore, greater accountability, which forces you to think, pushes you to ponder, and challenges your ignorance. We are not really talking about *surviving* on the plane of existence one day at a time; we are really talking about soaring beyond existence one day to come. Do you know the *complete* prayer?"

Wally looked puzzled. "You mean there is more to it?"

"Yes," replied Mentor. "It dates back at least to ancient times. More recently, Reinhold Niebuhr recovered and discussed it. Here is one variation:

God, grant me serenity to accept the things I cannot change,
Courage to change the things I can change,
and wisdom to know the difference.
Living one day at a time,
Enjoying one moment at a time,
Accepting hardship as a pathway to peace,
Taking, as Jesus did, this sinful world as it is,
Not as I would have it,
Trusting that you will make all things right,
If I surrender to your will,
So that I may be reasonably happy in this life
And supremely happy with you forever in the next.[1]

"Do you see the difference? The prayer as we know it is simply a vehicle to survive the plane of existence—to endure, persist, or survive with a basic quality of life. What is missing is a final *destination*. The pilgrim band is going to a specific destination; the twelve-step group is not really going anywhere in particular. Participants simply want to stay sober, clean, or free of addiction, but what they do after that, where they go after that, is unimportant. In the original prayer, the destination is supremely important. It is really a desire to transcend existence and unite with the infinite. Unfortunately, you cannot do that alone, nor even with the support of a peer group. Only the intentional intersection of the infinite can make this possible."

"What, then, is the final core prayer?" asked Antonia.

"The final prayer you compose anew every time you use this discipline. It is intercessory prayer specifically for absolute strangers. It is not prayer for yourself or for anyone you know. It is prayer solely and specifically for those you do not know. I urge you to begin with those strangers you have chanced to encounter in the last hour, then the last day, and then work outward in time to the last time you walked through the Hope Rosary. Of course, you rarely know any names. Your prayer is simply to picture the person, recall the situation, discern the need, or even the bare neutrality of their existence."

"Why should that matter?"

"I understand your skepticism," Mentor replied. "You are a surgeon. You are surrounded with unexpected death and inexorable illness even while families pray for safety and healing. You see unexpected life and unreasonable health when no one at all has prayed. That is the problem with both good and evil—it seems so gratuitous, undeserved, and random. Of what possible use can intercessory prayer be? And yet there is the compulsion to pray. This is the intersection of the infinite and the finite. The very *unpredictability* of life points to such an intersection. If there were no intersection, existence would merely be inexorable and perhaps unendurable. It is the uncertainty that drives us mad, but also that keeps us going. It is the infinite saying 'Maybe…maybe not.'

"And if we participate in that infinite unpredictability, could we possibly influence the outcome? Would compassion help? At the very least, this core prayer of intercession for strangers makes you sensitive to the intersection of the power of being and the depth of being. You begin to look for hidden experiences of infinite beginnings and intimate beginnings. It is a mystery, but it is also a mystery *in which you participate.* Hence, you pray."

"Careful!" The sudden cry startled the group. The mentor had been looking outward and had seen the toddler reaching out for the steaming drink while her mother was distracted by the cashier. A deft movement, muttered reproof, a glance of exasperated appreciation, and tragedy was avoided. Mentor stared at the scene a split second longer than necessary, apparently memorizing the tableau for later.

"The next bead," he said, "is again a single bead. This is the only passage of scripture explicitly used in the Hope Rosary. It is the famous "Fear not" passage from Isaiah 41:10:

> Fear not! For I am with you. Be not afraid! For I am your God. I will strengthen you; I will help you; I will uphold you with my victorious right hand!

"This is a necessary transition from the core prayers to the next stage of introspection. Fear is the enemy of all meditation. Many think that *distraction* is the enemy, but that is nothing. It is human to be distracted. We just concentrate all the more. Fear, however, blocks meditation entirely. Often, a 'distraction' is simply a tool of our fear. It is not that something else is more interesting, but that what we are about to see may be so alarming."

Mentor looked into the eyes of the people sitting around him in the café. "What do you fear?"

Each spoke of his or her fear. I was impressed at how seriously they took the question and how deliberately they sought to answer. Calvin, the social worker, feared cruelty and injustice; Antonia, the lawyer, feared reprisal. Bill, the businessman, feared poverty and impotence...and so on around the circle.

"Interesting, is it not, that the professions we choose and the careers we follow have more to do with addressing our fears than with achieving our hopes? Look deeper into your fears. Fundamentally, *we fear three things*. We fear death and the nameless fate that lies in wait for us. We fear meaninglessness and the futility of living. And we fear condemnation when our hidden inadequacies are brought to light and our guilt is revealed. All other fears are aspects of these three anxieties. We panic. We lose control. We flee. We create our own distractions simply to avoid facing 'the truth.'"

"But is it 'the truth'? The infinite is not indifferent to the finite. The infinite confronts these anxieties. 'Fear not!' Death, futility, and condemnation are not the last words of existence. *This hope is what precipitates three responding acts of courage.* I have said before that the infinite expresses itself in three ways: through Kairos, Logos, and Mythos. The existential implication of Kairos is that we can have courage to confront death, experience infinite beginnings, and risk relationship with others. The existential implication of Logos is that we can have courage to confront meaninglessness, uncover the logic of mind and nature, and risk self-affirmation. The existential implication of Mythos is that we can have courage to confront guilt, reenact patterns of meaning, and risk accepting acceptance."

"Mentor, this is Bill speaking. How do we know you are right? Why should we believe that the infinite cares about the finite? Skepticism is not only reasonable, but inevitable. We have no certainty that what you promise as hopeful might actually be true. Pragmatically speaking, the hope you offer is a bad investment, an opiate of the people, or a psychological evasion. Call it what you will. The evidence of history is against it."

"Truth is larger than evidence. That is the mistake of modernity, with all its scientific empiricism and pragmatic behavior. Truth is discerned through intuition as well. You may deduce facts, but you intuit meaning. In the intimate beginnings of life—birth, friendship, sex, marriage, aesthetic impression, intellectual insight, athletic timing, even scientific discovery—you intuit an order, purpose, and unity of being that is greater that the sum of the parts."

Bill still looked skeptical.

"Skepticism," the mentor continued, "assumes a world of external relations. This is the world of Newtonian physics and the Industrial Age. Skepticism assumes that all that is can be broken down into constituent parts, analyzed, manipulated, and reassembled (possibly with improvements by the ego that runs the assembly line). Skepticism perceives people and objects as data bytes coded into a grand computer; but the skeptic himself remains aloof, distant, apart, separated from life. Skeptics view life as a billiard table. The balls impact one another in infinite variation, and one simply needs to calculate the angles to survive. If one's competence to calculate the angles fails or if the game is prolonged too long, the frustrated or aging skeptic becomes a rebellious and crusty cynic." Mentor nodded at Bill. "And isn't that the real reason why your marriage failed and you divorced?"

"How did you know I am in the process of getting a divorce?" Bill asked surprised.

"Because all skeptics divorce in the end," Mentor replied. "Skepticism is the very principle of 'divorce.' That's the definition. One 'divorces' one's spouse (legally, spiritually, sexually, or relationally), just as the skeptic eventually 'divorces' all relationships (family, friendship, career, and any values-laden relationship), because fundamentally life is merely a collection of data bytes in temporary interaction with one another. Skeptics are lonely people." Mentor paused to observe a woman walking her dog outside the window. "They also make excellent pet owners," he mused. "Sentimentality is the antidepressant skeptics most commonly take."

"Antonia speaking…Mentor, are you saying, then, that life and religion depend on *internal* relations? That faith and belief and hope are possible only in a different perception of the world?"

"Yes, indeed. The intuition of our intimate beginnings leads us to the conclusion that all life is *internally connected.* No one thing is completely separated from another; no one person from another. Each individual participates in the internal constitution of everything else. All things (objects, people) participate in a greater order that is revealed in every 'form' or 'manifestation' of being. The ancients referred to this as *Logos.* Such internal relationships make skepticism impossible, because one simply does not and cannot sever the ego from everything else. There is no vantage point where one can view all the balls on the table, or the table itself, from a position of privileged isolation. This is most readily apparent in our intimate beginnings; but once that intuition rises to consciousness, it is apparent in life itself. This is why the ancient metaphor of *Logos* was 'word.' It did not mean the abstraction of a noun, but the action of a verb. The word was not a written word, but a spoken word. It is the basic component of conversation and, therefore, of relationship. Conversation 'creates' relationship. *Logos* creates 'life.'"

"Remember me? I'm Wally—an engineer. I never took a liberal arts course that I could avoid. Imagine I am designing and constructing a bridge. I am not going to talk that bridge into existence. I am going to design it according to the laws of physics and build it with raw materials. Then I and the construction crew will leave for another project. Millions of cars will drive over that bridge, and nobody will really care who built it. All they will care about is that the builders were competent. There are no 'internal relationships' here. Life, in the end, is just applied science. If I am able to believe the words 'Fear not, for I am with you' (and I'm not sure I can), then it might be in the context of being seriously ill or in my next tour of duty with the Army Reserve; but it won't occur to me in the building of that bridge."

Mentor nodded understandingly and paused to drink his coffee. Then he fixed his eyes on Wally. "In that case," he said, "eventually you will not be able to believe the words 'Fear not' in the hospital or the on battlefield either. It's all or nothing. Either the infinite is present in the finite everywhere and at all times, or the infinite is present in the finite nowhere and not at any time. If you cannot experience an internal relationship with the bridge—and with the millions of motorists crossing that bridge—then you will not experience the internal relationships in the hospital and on the battlefield. Your 'applied science' will eventually render you skeptical there, also. The hospital will become another complex structure, and you will worry about the doctor's competency. The battlefield will become merely a combination of morale and logistics, and you will worry about the general's competency.

"Let us take your example of building a bridge—perhaps the Golden Gate Bridge, or perhaps a simple footbridge over a creek, or perhaps a bridge to the stars, like Stonehenge. First, you have to imagine that bridge, picture its ideal function and purpose. Your labor will be motivated by the benefits that bridge will bring. Order and beauty will merge. Your personality will be embedded into the construction. You will not just 'walk away' to another project. You will smash a champagne bottle, drink a toast, take a photograph, and talk about it with the pride of accomplishment and the satisfaction of contributing to a larger purpose. No matter how good the bridge is, you will know its little imperfections and consider how you could have done better. Beneath the applied science is a depth of reason that is larger and more perfect than the bridge. The bridge only approximates it. This depth of reason extends as a web of relationship throughout your life—from the construction site, to the battlefield, and on to the hospital room. Each experience is an approximation of a deeper perfection. Each is an aspect of a greater order. Ancient engineers were like Magi—their best creations were attuned to the depth of reason that was beyond their competence but in which they participated."

"Nevertheless," Wally replied, still sifting through the implications of being internally connected to the ideal of "Bridge," "why should that make me believe that God is serious about saying 'Fear not'? Even if I am an internal participant in the depth of reason, why should I dare to think I can be a potential recipient of the power of God?"

"The intuition of our internal relationship with all things may be revealed through our *intimate* beginnings, but the intuition of our internal relationship with divinity comes through our experience of *infinite* beginnings. A few moments ago Bill asked, 'Why should we believe that the infinite cares about the finite?' Personally, I am cautious about using the verb *cares*, because to the modern mind it suggests 'care giving' alone, as if the intervention of the infinite in the finite must always be merciful or comforting. I think not. I think the experience of infinite beginnings may be cataclysmic, upsetting, and even painful. It may be death or life, devouring fire or the water of life. Yet however infinite beginnings are experienced, they do occur. They may not always be 'miracles.' They may be 'disasters.' Yet they do occur, and through them we intuit a Higher Power that is not indifferent to existence."

A tremendous din and confusion outside interrupted our conversation. Sirens blared, and fire trucks roared by, followed by an ambulance and police car. For a moment the entire intersection outside was absolute chaos as cars swerved out of the way, pedestrians ran to see what was happening, and everyone in the café burst into speculation. Obviously, someone's life had just taken a dramatic turn from the expected. After a few minutes, life resumed its pace, with everyone suddenly reminded of the fragility of normality.

"As I was saying," resumed the mentor, "the infinite is not indifferent to the finite. Why? The most obvious reason is that the network of internal relations that we experience as the depth of being also connects the finite and the infinite. God, you might say, is no more isolated from the world than one person is from another. The infinite and the finite are connected, just as the ideal perfection of 'Bridge' is connected to the imperfect manifestation of 'bridge.' It is this assumption that lies behind the creation of Stonehenge, but also the great cathedrals of Europe and the stone heads and human images erected by ancient people from the Antarctic to the Pacific Rim. People hope to follow the network that leads from the intricacy of form to the mystery of essence.

"Yet a less obvious, but even more significant, reason explains why the infinite is not indifferent to the finite. The finite is not just connected to the infinite. This connection is the *intention* of the infinite. The finite flows from the infinite; existence is created by God, as it were, as a fulfillment of God himself. God is no less interested in existence than a mother is interested in her child. Earlier I said that reducing truth to mere evidence is the failure of modernity, but I would add that limiting truth to intuition is the failure of postmodernity. Truth acts on its own. It pursues us relentlessly and independently of our willing participation. Truth encroaches on existence all the time. We tend to limit our understanding of truth to our asking questions of the infinite. In so doing we fail to see that the real power of truth lies in the infinite's questioning us. Life is an interrogation—a cross-examination, if you will—by God."

Maria looked pensive, and finally spoke. "Remember, I'm Maria. I think I am beginning to grasp what you are trying to say. I have been following the star diagram, which illustrates how simultaneously the finite reaches up to the infinite and the infinite reaches down to the finite. You are saying that the finite—humanity, you and me—intuits the infinite through intimate beginnings. We reach out to explore and unite with the infinite, but under the conditions of existence we inevitably find struggle, turmoil, confusion, doubt, and even death. And so we also search for clues, spiritual guides, mentors, and midwives who can somehow lead us through the ambiguities of existence toward the infinite. Is that right?"

Mentor nodded encouragingly.

"You are also saying that as we reach out from our intimate beginnings, so also the infinite—God—reaches down through our experiences of infinite beginnings, which are like life-changing crises."

"These are called moments of *Kairos,*" replied Mentor. They are occasions of being turned upside down and inside out, when being as we know it is suddenly reshaped to become a new being. Life is never quite the same again."

"But what is the impact of this?" asked Maria. "I mean, what is the effect of God's reaching down into existence?"

"The power of being intersects the depth of being," Mentor replied, "and the beneficial result is both order and meaning. On the one hand, the infinite imparts reasonable order on what would otherwise be utter chaos. *Logos* is the very possibility of reason, thought, reflection, and decision. It makes it possible for Wally to build the bridge, for example; but it also makes it possible for Wally's bridge to be compared with the perfection of 'Bridge.' The infinite makes Wally's applied science possible—and judges that applied science at the same time. On the other hand, the infinite imparts meaning patterns on what otherwise would be mere survival. *Mythos* is the very possibility of purposefulness, value, worth, and continuity. It makes it possible for Wally's bridge to expand commerce, culture, peace, and justice—and judges any limitation or failure of that bridge to accomplish these things at the same time."

"What I don't understand—me, Calvin—is why existence is so rotten. I mean, if the finite contains intimations of the infinite and if the infinite intends to reunite with the finite, then why don't we live in a perfect world? Instead of justice, we have injustice. Instead of health, we have sickness. Instead of reason, we have violence. Instead of internal relations, we have war. This entire conversation has been about whether we can really believe the words 'Fear not,' but I ask a different question: Why do we have to believe them at all? Why does God have to speak them? Why do we have to fear anything in the first place and so have to be reassured? Why are we left here yearning, unable to experience fulfillment? What's wrong with existence, that the intersection between the finite and the infinite has become such a mess?"

"I'm Debra. Before the mentor speaks, let me share my 'take' on the predicament we are in, based on my perceptions of the educational system. The problem lies in our choices. Even when we understand our options, we all too consistently *choose* to behave selfishly. Existence is a mess because people choose unwisely. Egos get in the way. Self-interest takes over. You see it among students, amid corporations, and between nations. People are not only stupid, but they prefer it that way. Education helps, but in the end, people choose what is good for the individual instead of what is good for the globe. So we're in a mess; we have plenty to fear; and it is encouraging to hear God say 'Fear not!'"

"I think you are right, Debra, but I don't think we are yet to the core of the problem. We experience the infinite *under the conditions of existence.* Plato might say it is like staring at shadows; Paul might say it is like looking in a clouded mirror. But what exactly are the 'conditions of existence' that block the achievement of the just society, a healthy environment, or however we picture the perfect world? If it is stupidity, then people can be educated. It may take a long time and require new technologies and methodologies, but progress can be made. If it is selfish choices, then people can be persuaded. Again, it may take a long time, require acts of 'tough love,' and barely escape environmental Armageddon; but progress can still be made, and we can hope for a breakthrough. Yet I think the *conditions of existence* are rather more problematic than this, or we would have seen more progress in human history than we have."

"Surely you are not going to talk about 'original sin,'" Maria interrupted. "It's taken me twenty years to get over the hang-ups and low self-esteem my parents embedded into my psyche that were designed to 'keep me in my place' in society. I'm not about to go back now!"

The mentor drained his coffee cup—and choked on the grounds left at the bottom. One of our group leapt up to thump him on the back. Eventually he cleared his throat, tears still wet on his cheeks, and smiled. "Thank you," he said. "My pride would not be able to endure the ignominy of 'death by coffee.'" He turned back to Maria.

"Yet that is the condition of our existence. Death is implicit in life, and there is nothing we can do about it. Stand silent in any cemetery. Did these people die heroically or ignominiously? No one knows. Eventually, no one cares."

"That's it?" Maria asked. "So we accept that eventually all must die. It comes one day to us all. But until then, we can live nobly or poorly, wisely or stupidly, generously or selfishly. And perhaps if we are good enough, disciplined enough, or knowledgeable enough, our soul can unite with the infinite; and we will live forever."

"You speak as if 'death' were a force beyond yourself, or as if 'death' were a reality yet to come at the end of life. Death is not the end of life. Death is a part of life—inextricably bound up with life. Death is the dark side of every good decision, or the unspoken negation of every affirmation. Death is the constant 'either/or' in a life we desperately want to be 'both/and.' 'If this…then not that.' You assume 'now I live, then I will die'; but I say that you are already dying. The tentacles of death entangled you from birth. Your every breath, your every act, and your every joke are tainted by this corruption of life.

"They say survival is a primal instinct; is it not so? Do you not see this over and over again in the hospital? on the street? in business? in courts of law?" He looked at Maria, Calvin, Bill, and Antonia in turn. "It is pure, unadulterated, undiluted finitude. Greed, lust, envy, anger, gluttony, and laziness are just exaggerations of elaborate self-defense to ensure the survival of our selfhood. But so also are generosity, prudence, respect, mercy, asceticism, and discipline aspects of the same instinct to preserve the self. A hidden selfishness lies behind all philanthropy, as well as behind all criminality. The ancients called that 'pride';   early Christians called it the 'original sin.' The difference about this 'sin,' however, is that you can do nothing whatsoever about it. This sin is the tentacle of death."

"But I want to unite with the infinite. I don't want to preserve my 'self' at all costs. I am prepared to do whatever it takes, discipline myself in any way, so that I might surrender utterly to the infinite!" Calvin was too moved to remember to identify himself. "I am so weary of trying to do good and always falling short. I am so tired of laboring for justice and always being beaten by injustice; exhausting myself for wholeness, only to see more brokenness." One could see Antonia and Maria nodding imperceptibly.

"*You* want it, do you? *Calvin* wants it. *Calvin* is tired and exhausted. That is the paradox again, the condition of existence. *Calvin* wants to merge with the infinite—but merging with the infinite means that what *Calvin wants* is no longer relevant. Are you able to give up 'wanting' anything? You *want* perfection. Justice is *preferable* to injustice, and wholeness is *preferable* to brokenness. You *want* these things, but the fact of 'desire,' 'preference,' and 'choice' is what defines the very 'self' you would surrender. The condition of existence is not 'I think, therefore I am,' but 'I am…and there is nothing I can do about it.'"

"I could kill myself," Calvin said quietly, hesitantly, fearfully. "If this trap of existence is so complete that my very attempts for justice and wholeness carry within themselves the seeds of injustice and brokenness, perhaps that is the only solution. That, or total abandonment to selfishness. I cannot overcome death; and therefore, I cannot overcome pride. Taking my own life—accelerating my own death—might be the best and finest and angriest protest I can make. My name *is* Calvin, and there is nothing else I can really do about it."

Silence gripped the entire group. Indeed, the café itself had gone suddenly quiet. Calvin's emotion could not be ignored. The intensity of his words, if not the volume of his voice, carried all the way to the serving line at the counter. People hesitated a step on their way out the door, and newcomers looked puzzled at the gloom they felt upon entering. They looked about, thinking that they had just missed something, while the people exiting looked back relieved to be just escaping something. Neither knew what it was.

"However," said Mentor slowly, "the infinite is not indifferent to the finite. It may be that there is nothing you can do about the conditions of existence, at least not fundamentally. That does not imply that there is no hope. The ground of our hope must lie elsewhere than in the educational, therapeutic, or creative actions of the finite. If the intersection of the infinite and the finite reveals the conditions of existence all too starkly, that same intersection can reveal the possibilities within existence with equal clarity. What we need is a singular experience of 'both/and' that can shatter the trap of 'either/or.'"

With that rather enigmatic statement, Mentor left.

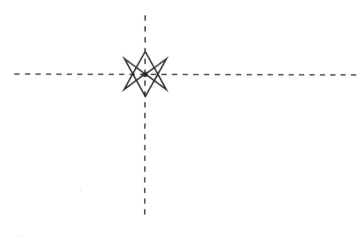

Second Dialogue

I found him again in the food court at the local shopping mall. Once again he sat in a corner, with a group gathered around him, many of whom I recognized from the café, but with many newcomers as well. As before, people tended to come and go, although a core group clearly lingered for animated conversation. As before, the rule about identifying oneself before speaking was in play. This time the mentor was sipping a tall smoothie instead of coffee. Perhaps, I thought, he remembered the incident with the coffee grounds.

The Teaching

"Mentor? Remember me? I am Debra. The last time we spoke, you were introducing us to the spiritual discipline of the Hope Rosary, as you called it. You guided us through the discipline of the cross pendant and the first beads of the chain until you were sidetracked by our discussion about 'fear' and 'hope.' Will you please continue?"

Mentor nodded thoughtfully. "Of course. However, I do not think we were sidetracked in our last conversation, because I think what was said very much needed to be said. The initial beads on the Hope Rosary—the initial steps in this spiritual discipline—are intended to bring you to the basic predicament of existence. They are intended to prompt fundamental questions, desires, crises, anxieties, and so on. The last bead we discussed, reminding us of the 'Fear not' passage from the prophet Isaiah, offers both assurance and challenge. How do we actually go about 'living fearlessly'? How does one live into hope on a daily basis?"

"I'm Wally. Remember me?"

"I do remember you, Wally." The exchange, by now, had made a ritual of recognition. They made eye contact, as if each brought back whole files of previous interaction.

"You have touched on my precise question. Ever since our last conversation, I have been swept away by the obligations and pleasures of real living. It is one thing—and yes, it is a good thing—to ponder these issues of life and death. And although it may be that *all* experiences are 'life-and-death' experience, the truth is that only *some* experiences are really felt in that way. Mostly, life goes on (or at least *my* life goes on) on a more moderate level."

"Yes—I'm Bill, and I absolutely agree. The instant I left the café last time and turned on my cell phone, I felt as if I had immersed myself in a maze of ordinariness. Most of my time was reactive; some of my time was proactive; but all of my time was pressured. Within hours, I felt lost again. If the infinite was not indifferent to my experience of the finite, I sure couldn't tell."

Mentor nodded understandingly. "Therefore, the next step in the Hope Rosary is to hold the central medallion in one's hand to meditate on daily life and orient oneself to the infinite. The medallion is a kind of compass; or, if you will, the talisman is a kind of global positioning device in the chaos of ordinariness that engulfs you. A typical rosary medallion bears the image of Jesus on one side and the Virgin Mary on the other. This does make sense to me, because in the end it is the experience of incarnation that focuses the intersection of the infinite and finite. However, my medallion bears the star graphic that has become so familiar to you. This is the diagram of intersecting triangles illuminating the plane of existence."

The mentor turned a paper placemat over and quickly drew the following diagram, so familiar to us who had read and discussed his philosophy:

He continued. "The spiritual discipline of the Hope Rosary bids you hold the medallion and reflect on your present location in relationship to the six foci of essence and existence. The dot in the middle represents the truly centered self, but the reality is that at any given moment we are not there. We are elsewhere on the map, and often in movement toward another location on the map. Your meditation can help you take control of that movement. At the very least, you can take steps to place yourself in the way of God, and you might even be able to direct yourself toward the will of God."

"You mean to say—I'm Debra—that at one point I may find myself embroiled in some conflict, stress, or other life struggle and that if I can reflect on that experience in conjunction with the larger 'map,' I can anticipate a way out. For example, I might focus on seeing some pattern of meaning or learning that will give purpose to the struggle, or I might search for reasonable solutions to resolve the struggle, or I might simply surrender to a 'Higher Power' to break me out of that struggle."

"Yes," Mentor replied. "As you see on the map, the most 'direct' route to centering yourself would be to discern purpose or meaning in the midst of life struggle, but that may not be possible. Perhaps you go sideways in one direction or another."

"Perhaps for me—Bill—" contributed another voice, "I might find myself locked into a routine that has lost meaning, or a self-image or stage in life that is restrictive and unhappy. It would be a negative way to experience a 'meaning pattern' or 'myth.' And I need to throw myself into some new challenge or place myself beyond my comfort zones in an unfamiliar environment, precipitating struggle and forcing me out of the expected. Sort of like when I dropped out of business for a year to go build orphanages in Guatemala."

"Yes," Mentor replied. "You might also have sought out a spiritual coach to guide you through your depression or initiated a sexual affair with another woman." Bill winced, but said nothing. "Within limits, you can take responsibility for your spiritual growth. At other times, the infinite will precipitate you into change, whether you like it or not."

So far we had been oblivious to the confusion and noise of the food court, but the sudden wailing of a small child and the raised voice of an adult intruded on us. We all paused to stare as the couple emerged from the discount store. "No, no, no! Don't touch!" the woman was saying in a most threatening and intimidating manner. The child tugged and pulled and complained as they walked away down the mall. This time, a number of the group appeared to be making a mental note for future prayer or pondering, and not a few glanced at the star diagram hastily scratched on the place mat.

"This is Antonia. Can you give me an example of how you would find your way on the map out of an experience of Kairos?"

Mentor drank deeply as he considered. "We might begin by quoting Paul: 'If I speak in the tongues of mortals and of angels, but do not have love, I am a noisy gong or a clanging cymbal [1 Cor. 13:1, NRSV]." Kairos is often equated with 'spiritual gifts' or 'charismata' that suddenly invade or overwhelm a person's rationality and individuality. The apostle says these experiences are worthless unless (as you see from the star diagram) they are connected to intimacy. This is why the passage is a favorite at weddings, because it connects the experience of 'falling in love' with the experience of 'being in love.'

"But there is a good deal more to it than that! Kairos moments are not necessarily dramatic, emotional, or even particularly noteworthy experiences in themselves. The point is that the infinite can seize any moment, no matter how mundane, and transform it into an experience that changes a life. Kairos is an experience of *infinite beginning*. It is always unexpected and always apocalyptic to the individual. It is as if Bill were to go to the water cooler and come back a changed man; or as if Wally were to see a spider's web for the millionth time—and yet truly see it for the first time—and the insight changed his career."

Wally picked up the reference. "This in a way is precisely what happened to attract me to a career as an engineer. Only it wasn't a spider's web," he said blushing. "It was Legos."

Antonia responded. "If I follow correctly, then, the most direct way toward the centered self is to move from *infinite* beginning (Kairos) to *intimate* beginnings. Or I might move sideways to seek out spiritual guidance to interpret the experience…"

"And if you do neither," Bill interjected, "the Kairos moment simply disrupts your life altogether, and you place yourself in a life struggle the likes of which you have never known before!" Mentor looked at him. "I'm Bill," he added.

At this point Mentor looked away, and we could see that he was observing the same mother and child returning down the mall. This time they were quiet, holding hands. The child was eating something contentedly, while the mother admired the store windows. "I wonder where they are on the star graphic," someone in our group mused quietly. Mentor picked up on the quiet voice and responded to the question. "We may not ever know, because we haven't enough information. But does the mother know? If so, she will be better able to guide her child as he grows up. If not, if the change was simply accidental or if she does not reflect more deeply about guiding her child, then both mother and child will find themselves easily lost in the complexities of their future."

"Mentor, remember me? I'm Maria. As simple as the star diagram is, I actually find it difficult to apply. The different foci of the star seem to blend into one another. Is there a meditative technique that can more readily help me locate myself in life?"

"Yes, there is. As you hold the medallion in your hand, cast your mind back to the immediate past (the past day or week). There are three 'ways of being,' and to a degree we may participate in all three at once. Yet as we focus on each way of being, we can study the flow of our experience as life-on-the-edge, or life-in-between, and occasionally as life-at-peace. We will, of course, pass through the medallion twice as we follow the circular chain of beads. At this first passage, I suggest you focus solely on the first two ways of being as the most logical step following the act of courage to 'Fear not.' We will reflect on the third way of being as we finish the Hope Rosary."

The food court was now beginning to fill for the lunch hour. The leisurely shoppers and relaxed retirees were now overbalanced by hurried business people, raucous teens, couriers, truck drivers, travelers, retailers on break, and preoccupied twenty–somethings on a quest for something. These newcomers hurriedly scooped up sandwiches. Whereas women had dominated the food court when we arrived, now there was an equal mix of men. The median age had clearly gone down. The music became louder now. The vendors raised their voices to be heard and to market their wares.

"In general," Mentor said with a smile, "it would seem that our environment has passed from life-in-between to life-on-the-edge. The sound level is higher, the movement more frantic, the eye contact more urgent, and the pulse rates for most of the people seem to be higher." He gestured to the pizza stalls. "I perceive courtship rituals—patterns of subtle meaning communicated in the behavior of the teenagers preening to attract the attention of the opposite sex."

"And over there," Bill remarked, adding hastily "Bill here." He was looking at the coffee bar that attracted a more mature and sophisticated clientele. "The mating rituals are just more subtle."

"You're eyesight is all too keen," sighed Mentor, but he turned his attention to Maria. "Of course, while the environment itself may seem on-the-edge, no doubt the people in this microcosm of life are all over the map. Do I need to explain these ways of being more fully?" Maria nodded.

"Everyone experiences life-on-the-edge, although some may invite it more than others, and some may resist it more than others. It is our investment in experimentation. It is risk. It is vulnerability. The moment you consider looking for a new job or find yourself attracted to a person of the opposite sex or simply form a new friendship or invest in a new suit of clothes or buy a new book, you are experimenting with something different in various degrees of urgency. It does not have to feel as radical as an extreme sport or a dramatic change of life direction. The cumulative effect is to feel 'edgy'—excited, stressed, eager, or anxious. The faster and more unpredictable life becomes, the more we must risk and experiment to adapt, the more vulnerable we feel, and the more on-the-edge becomes a dominant way of being."

Maria nodded again. "It's the story of my life," she said. "I hate it."

"Actually, I think you both hate and love it," Mentor replied, "or you would not have chosen to be a surgeon. Life-on-the-edge is an experience of love/hate ambiguity, and of strong pulls in seemingly opposite directions. This is why, when you use the star graphic for meditation, it is helpful to approach it through the lens of reflection about your life on-the-edge. You look at 'oppositions' on the diagram. For example, examine your life in the opposition of infinite beginnings and intimate beginnings. Intimacy blossoms quickly in the urgency of 'edginess' and provokes new experiences of the infinite. On the other hand, the infinite erupts quickly in environments of experimentation and risk and can shatter even our most intimate relationships. It is no accident that divorce and remarriage is more common among professions lived on-the-edge."

"I'm Debra, and I understand how life struggle and meaning patterns can be perceived as opposites, so that life-on-the-edge can be simultaneously drawn to both radical freedom and radical submission. I see it among teens in my high school all the time. One day they rebel against everything and everyone, and the next day they surrender all autonomy to another marketing scheme or cult hero. I am less clear on how the opposition between Logos (reasonable order) and spiritual coaching is experienced."

"It is the opposition between linear and lateral, right brain and left brain, inexorable logic and gut intuition. Viewed with rigorous logic, the world (and one's life) can be ordered into strict, pragmatic patterns of reason, but the end result is ambiguity rather than clarity. Life cannot be contained by reason. Those whose lives are on-the-edge cannot live by logic alone or by knowledge alone. Thus, they search beyond themselves for mentors or guides who can help them discover a larger synthesis. In reverse, the intuition of the spiritual guide requires the rigor of reason, or it becomes lost in fantasy and imagination.

"I hope you will excuse the generalization, but this is the core dilemma of public education at the end of the modern era. Teens are living on-the-edge as never before in a society of speed, flux, and blur. The response of modernity is to offer more knowledge or to impose reasonable order, assuming that if youth just had better curriculum and better teachers, all would be well. Their need, however, is not more teachers, but better mentors or spiritual guides. They provide not more knowledge, but coaching in the use of that knowledge and guidance to synthesize that knowledge into a larger hope."

The mentor again stared out at the mayhem of the food court. We had to lean closer to hear one another. "Observe the more visible police presence," he said. "You see uniforms over there, but I think that is mainly a diversion to distract people from the plainclothes security standing so observantly over there. The typical modern response to mayhem is the imposition of authority to 'keep order,' when what is needed is some form of spiritual guidance to 'coach meaning.'"

"Mentor, it's me, Calvin. Although people make much of our constantly changing world and the stress of living on-the-edge, my perception is actually very different. I see the world as remarkably, tragically, unchanging. Routine dominates life. Life is much the same day in and day out. That may be comforting to some, but it is grindingly depressing to others. I think much of the behavior we associate with 'life-on-the-edge' is mere pretense, as if we are convincing ourselves that we are not, in fact, crushed by the constant sameness of living."

"I agree, Calvin." Mentor looked thoughtfully at a gang of brassy twelve–year-olds passing by our tables. "The reality is that only a smaller percentage of our lives are lived on-the-edge, although it may feel like the norm. Much of our life is lived 'in-between'—the second way of being.

Life-in-between is the experience of ambiguity itself, or of being caught between moments of change. Such moments may be so far apart that life seems utterly routine, monotonous, or dull. But they may also be experiences of expectancy, waiting, watching, hoping, and enduring. Life-in-between is an experience of frustrated persistence or comfortable existence. It is sometimes confused with life-at-peace, but it would be more accurate to describe it as the current absence of violence. Life is still stressful. Indeed, more heart attacks occur when life is in-between than when life is on-the-edge." He was looking now at a group of seniors that had been idling away the entire morning at a table nearby.

"How are we to interpret life-in-between using the star diagram?"

"Think 'apposites' rather than 'opposites,'" he replied. So deep was his reverie that he forgot to ask the questioner's name. "In other words, your next move when life is in-between is to look to either side on the diagram. In the experience of intimate beginnings, you move laterally to invest it with patterns of meaning or to understand it with rational analysis. Or in the experience of life struggle, you either analyze the scientific or sociological reasons for the crisis or you pray for a moment of Kairos. Or in the uncertainty brought by absence of spiritual insight, you open yourself to unexpected inspiration or surrender yourself to ritual habits."

"This is Calvin. What you are saying is that the basic response to life-in-between is to leverage some kind of movement, some kind of transition, which will take you from the status quo and change the environment in which you live or think?"

"Yes. It may not be as dramatic a change as life-on-the-edge, but it is change nonetheless. Somehow, to grow and to have hope, you must introduce some change into your life."

"I notice that when you talk about apposites in life-in-between, you always refer to the experience of *intimate beginnings, life struggles,* or *spiritual coaching* as the center from which you look side to side. Why? Why not also center on *Kairos, Logos,* or *Mythos* and look side to side from there? I'm Debra."

"Life-on-the-edge is precipitated by the direct interaction of the infinite and the finite. So we look across the star graphic for answers. Kairos and intimacy interact. Mythos and life struggle interact. Logos and spiritual coaching interact. Life-in-between is different. It is life lived squarely in the midst of daily experience, within the sole context of finitude. That is what makes life-in-between so routine, so subject to the inexorable passage of time. It is boring and comforting all at once, precisely because the infinite is not readily perceived or experienced. Therefore, we start at the place of our existence, but then look to infinite possibilities on either side. To leverage movement beyond the status quo (as Calvin puts it), we must somehow open ourselves to the possibility of the infinite. And the infinite is present to the finite in three basic ways: Kairos, Logos, or Mythos. The experience of any one of these can move us forward and give us hope."

For a time, the entire group fell silent, brooding, I think, on these foreign-sounding terms. The situation was really quite bizarre. Here was a group of ten professional people sitting in a food court. We were surrounded by the diversity of the public busily being as selfish, shallow, and indifferent as they possibly could be while we contemplated the meaning of Kairos, Logos, and Mythos.

"Yet it is not as shallow we might think," mused Mentor aloud, as if reading our thoughts. "Beneath a certain level of defensive superficiality, this environment teems with unanswered questions and desperate searching."

Antonia stirred to speak. "Mentor, how can one seek answers without a guide? The star diagram describes finitude reaching up from the depths of being. Intimate beginnings precipitate the experience of life struggle and the search for spiritual guides. Yet it seems to me that Life Struggle is a very broad description, whereas 'spiritual guide' is something very specific. Where would these people…" and she swept the food court at lunchtime with her hand "…find such a guide? What would they look for?"

"Every Dante needs his Beatrice if he is to explore the depths of hell and the heights of heaven," responded the mentor, smiling. "The quest for spiritual guidance is no mere tactic, but an instinct just as fundamental as the inevitability of life struggle. The 'guide' may come and go, but the need for 'guidance' endures. To find guides, you have only to look from side to side in the midst of life-in-between. Guidance may be for a fleeting moment, weeks of intentional conversation, or years of intermittent interaction. It may consist of speaking words or modeling behavior, and you may or may not even know the name of the guide."

"But what do they do? I'm Wally. And how can I tell an authentic guide apart from, say, some con artist or cult leader or proselytizing clergy?"

"The function of a spiritual guide is apparent in the star diagram as well. In the context of life-on-the-edge, spiritual guides bring reason and order to experience, but also intuition and insight that discerns a higher purpose to the logic of existence. Consider the great Aristotle. Simultaneously the innovator of natural science and the first to categorize species, he also became the mentor and ethical advisor to Alexander the Great. In the context of life-in-between, spiritual guides infuse order with meaning, leading people to either open themselves to Kairos or immerse themselves in Mythos. Spiritual guides are not therapists, and certainly not evangelists. Nor, I think, can they be 'trained' or 'licensed' or 'ordained' to the purpose, for I do not think any study program will make a spiritual guide. A spiritual guide is one who has 'been there, done that, and lived to tell about it' when it comes to life-on-the-edge and life-in-between."

"I'm Bill, remember? Let me ask a practical question. So, I am holding the central medallion of the Hope Rosary in my fingers, and I can feel the weight of the pendant cross beneath my hand, and I am thinking... what?"

"To what extent is my life—right now, this week—life-on-the-edge? Reflect on the *oppositions* of the star diagram as the infinite and finite interact with each other. Life struggle cries out for patterns of meaning; routine needs to be broken by struggle. Intimate beginnings draw one into infinite beginnings; Kairos shatters the comforts of living. Analysis seeks synthesis; intuition contradicts rationality. Brood on these things. To what extent is your life lived in-between?

"Reflect on the *oppositions*. These are both causes and possibilities. Life struggle is caught (and shaped) between inexorable law and apocalyptic change. Intimate beginnings are caught (and shaped) between reason and myth. Spiritual guidance, as we have seen, is caught (and shaped) between patterns of meaning and new being. Of course, one is often living both on-the-edge and in-between at the same time, and the proportion of energy devoted to each way of being may vary even from hour to hour. Nevertheless, in this discipline you can begin to locate yourself in the complex interaction of the finite and the infinite—and take the necessary next steps."

"What you are doing," Maria said shrewdly, "is forcing us to focus on the right questions. The discipline helps us clarify what are, or are not, the real issues facing us at any given time."

"Yes," replied Mentor, "but that is not to say that the answers may not then be apparent in the questions. The best and most focused questions always carry within themselves clues to the best and most relevant answers. This, in itself, is a sign of the internal participation of the finite and the infinite. The opposite is true as well. The best and most relevant answers always carry within themselves seeds to the next most urgent questions. The questions of the finite anticipate the answers of the infinite, and the answers of the infinite redefine the questions of the finite. That is what you are about as you meditate on the central medallion."

"Mentor, I'm Calvin. You have not spoken at any length about life-at-peace. Is this a genuine possibility? Or is it just a dream?"

"Life-at-peace is the third way of being, yes, and theoretically it would be perfectly appropriate to discuss it in the context of the other two. However, in the context of the spiritual discipline of the Hope Rosary, it is premature. Indeed, in the sense that we must first confront the other two ways of being *before* we can even hope to experience life-at-peace, it is better to postpone that conversation until we have explored further the infinite answers to finite questions."

At this point a sudden explosion of argument interrupted us. A vendor began trading shouts and profanities with a buyer. It was impossible to know the cause, or even how people were involved, but the dispute overcame all conversation in the food court. A crowd gathered quickly, either curious to know what was happening or eager to see a fight. The rapid appearance of a security guard, radio in hand, just as quickly dispersed the crowd and silenced the disputants. Within minutes the storm had receded, the buzz of innumerable conversations (I hesitate now to suggest they were *all* trivial) returned, and the normality of life-in-between was reestablished.

Mentor continued. "Perhaps it will be helpful to reflect together on the goal of the 'centered self.' Remember that central dot on the star diagram, in the middle of existence, and at the intersection of the infinite and the finite. Such perfect balance represents the centered self. Although it is the goal of everyone's reflection, it is difficult to achieve and perhaps impossible to maintain."

"Debra speaking. Would you compare life-at-peace to Buddhist descriptions of nirvana or mystical expressions of bliss?"

"Perhaps, and perhaps not. As I say, I think it is premature to consider such things until we have probed the intentionality of the infinite toward the finite. Instead, let us come at it in a different way and ask ourselves, 'What are the conditions necessary to achieve the centered self?' Our clues may be taken from the star graphic itself." The mentor began to count them on his fingers.

"First, the centered self must be one who knows the bitter experience of life struggle, victimization, and pain—and yet has overcome despair to connect that experience with a deeper meaning, purpose, and hope. That centered self would be able to transition from life struggle to surrender to infinite beginnings on the one hand, and rigorous reason on the other hand, without losing autonomy."

Mentor paused as we all sought to absorb this description and picture what such a centered self would look like.

"Second, the centered self must have experienced the deepest intimacy and vulnerability and know the sorrow of betrayal or loss. The centered self must have enjoyed life to the fullest but also have had life and relationship shattered by change, only to emerge again not only to survive but to thrive, as a new person, readily investing once again in the deepest intimacy, knowing full well the risks."

Again, we paused to digest this description of the centered self. Some revealed expressions of incredulity or frustration, and Calvin's expression betrayed a growing sense of hopelessness.

"Third, the centered self must merge reason and intuition, science and meaning. The centered self must have experienced the rigor of law and logic, knowing its power and limitations. This person has been both mentor and mentee. He or she can accept being speechless with fright or delight on the one hand and can interpret and model patterns of meaning on the other hand. The centered self is at once both philosopher and mystic."

Bill looked compassionately at crestfallen Calvin. "Then it is impossible," he said. "I'm Bill, and I perceive that at best we can approximate the centered self, but we cannot achieve it. Can anyone here imagine themselves being that person?"

Everyone in the group looked at one another and shook their heads. "Perhaps," said Debra, "if one sold everything, gave up career and family and home, and retired to a desert monastery to live in utter simplicity so as to shun all temptation, and found a wise guru to act as guide, one *might,* after much labor and sacrifice, center oneself."

"I do not think even that would work," replied Mentor. "Reducing the encumbrances of existence does not eliminate the conditions of existence. The monk can be as tempted by a morsel of bread as by a latte in the café. Moreover, if one isolates oneself from intimacy, how, then, can one truly know life struggle? or understand the quest for spiritual guidance? Most attempts to *achieve* the centered self result in journeying to the extremes of the map that is the star diagram. People shut themselves up in a laboratory or a monastery. They join a cult or abandon themselves to pleasure or self-pity. They retreat into dogmatism and fantasy or do nothing at all or everything at once. All this they do in the hope of *achieving* the centered self. All they really do is render themselves even more 'off balance' than they were in the first place."

"So has anyone done it?" asked Calvin.

"The question you should ask is not 'Has anyone done it?' but rather 'Has anyone gotten there?'" The mentor leaned forward encouragingly. "We are not quite ready to make any conclusions about the hope of the centered self until we reflect on the intentions of the infinite. What cannot be *achieved* might well be *given.* What we are really talking about with the description of centered self is *incarnation.* Can the infinite and finite be perfectly, paradoxically, united to create a paradigm for the centered self? Could that incarnation guide us toward the centered self? More importantly, could participation in that incarnation do for us what we cannot do by ourselves, bringing us to the reality of the centered self? This is why the next part of the Hope Rosary leads one to reflect on six more beads, each representing an aspect of incarnation. Each bead challenges us to consider the *intentionality* of the infinite that is not indifferent to the finite."

The final words were almost lost amid a new uproar in the food court, caused by workmen with handcarts delivering supplies, custodians cleaning floors, and one particularly grumpy waitress who had obviously decided that we had long overstayed our welcome occupying tables others required. She began wiping the tables with exasperated vigor, and we dispersed.

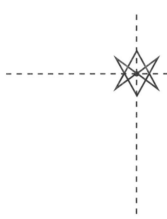

Third Dialogue

ECHO'S JOURNAL _

We had decided to meet on the boardwalk at the beach. It was very early in the morning. The amusement park down the beach was still silent, and even the vendors had not yet arrived to open their stalls. Stores remain closed, except for a few coffee shops and snow cone operators doing business with joggers, strollers, seniors, and not a few solitary middle-aged men or women looking at the ocean with various mixtures of meditation and melancholy. It was a perfect opportunity to talk before the busy workday.

We had expected only a few, but about fifteen of us were sitting around tables, on benches or beach chairs, or lying on the sand beyond the boardwalk. Word had spread of our meeting, and some had clearly invited friends or colleagues to listen. I gathered that Maria had invited another hospital worker, and Bill seemed to have brought someone from the office. Conversation started slowly as we admired our surroundings.

It was not only a beautiful moment, but one obviously provocative of deep reflection. The cool ocean breeze broke the clinging humidity. It promised to be a warm day, with typical thunderstorms later in the afternoon. For now, however, it was extraordinarily calm. I couldn't imagine any place more symbolic of the intersection of the infinite and the finite. (Such was the state of my mind and training that such words as *infinite* and *finite* came naturally to my thinking.) The ocean kissed the shore in little ripples, like a lover brushing her beloved's face with her lips, the wind from her breath scented and suggestive of the unknown. In the far distance clouds were already gathering, and from time to time you could see lighting flashes in her eyes.

A movement and a splash suggested erratic life that contradicted the predictable lapping of the waves, but never when you were looking for it. You felt an uncontrollable urge to kiss back—to feel the water through your hands, wade into wet, or sail into the unknown. You could see the odd sailboat, or hear the distant sputter of a motorboat, and instantly think, *"Yes, I want to be 'out there'; I want to leave everything and immerse myself in you!"* The jetties and piers along the beach became fingers and arms reaching out to embrace the infinite. Yet they were inevitably rusted or broken in failure.

It was still possible to look directly into the sun rising over the water, now a deep, unreflective yellow peering through her veil of humid air. Reflected light shot across the ocean like an arrow aimed at everyone and yet piercing each, single, individual, human heart. In my fantasy I heard a question posed and unanswered (or maybe it was a song from a distant radio): "Do you really want to love me? Do you really think your trinkets can buy my attention, or that your philosophies can encompass my emotion, or that your prayers can control my action?" Obviously not! And yet the ocean waves kept coming.

A polite cough broke the reverie, and everyone started to move. A few digital cameras were quietly put away, and I smiled to think of the number of digital photos that would soon be background and screensaver to the star diagram on various PDAs and computers.

Mentor began. "We have yet to complete the meditative discipline of the Hope Rosary. It takes far longer to explain than to do, and the more distant we are from antiquity and the more entrapped we are by modernity, the longer it takes to explain. At any rate, when we last talked, we discussed two of the three ways of being, life-on-the-edge and life-in-between, which our faith and courage had prepared us to address. Do you recall how we concluded?"

Wally responded the most quickly—perhaps the impact of his surroundings made him especially eager that day. "Remember me? Wally? We concluded that the conditions required for a truly centered life were nigh on impossible to achieve, but might be possible as an experience of grace."

"I do not think that I used the word *grace*. It is a good word, of course, but its association with various dogmas and mythologies of 'salvation' make it unsuitable to really describe the infinite that is *not indifferent* to the finite. Like so many dogmas, doctrines, ritual practices, and sacramental rites, the word *grace* implies an institutionalization of the participation of the infinite in the finite that is too limiting. In the context of the star graphic, the word *grace,* like the *church* itself, should really be associated with Logos and the quest for reasonable order, or Mythos and the quest for patterns of meaning. But it cannot really encompass the fullness of the intersection of the infinite and the finite. I prefer to use the word *generosity* to describe the inclination of the infinite to the finite. The infinite is generous—sometimes to the point of unpleasant or unexpected extremes. Let that suffice, and we can avoid needless sidetracks into theologies of this and that."

"But Mentor, *why* should the infinite be generous toward the finite? Remember me? I'm Maria. If we are to get behind (or perhaps leave behind) the various creation stories and mythologies from many religions, it still seems mysterious to me *why* the infinite should even bother with the finite? And to be even more specific, *why* should the infinite bother *about me?*"

"Love requires no rationale. But I think it is easy for modernity, shaped as it is by the limitations of science and Christendom, to mistake the nature of this love. The ancients spoke of three aspects of love: Friendship *(Phileos),* Sacrifice *(Agape),* and Desire *(Eros).* Scientific people tend to limit love to friendship, whereas churchy people tend to limit themselves to sacrificial acts. And truly, both aspects of love are important expressions of the infinite's generosity toward the finite. But I think the manner of love most descriptive of the mutual attraction of the infinite and the finite is *desire.*"

Mentor caught sight of a few flushed faces or humorous looks and smiled understandingly.

"Yes, the modern mind has been trained both by science and by religion to reduce *Eros* to 'sex.' But please get over it. *Eros,* or 'desire,' is the drive toward unity—the merging of one with another—the internal participation that connects the finite in one interrelated whole and reaches out to the infinite. The infinite 'desires' the finite, just as the finite 'desires' the infinite, for the sake of completeness. The creative act, whether it is the birth of an idea, the expression of art, or the innovation of a technology, is an experience of *Eros.* We create abstractions, concepts, and forms that may be pedantic or genius, but these are all imperfect anticipations of the infinite. In reverse, the finite itself is made up of abstractions, concepts, and forms that are all imperfect expressions of the infinite. The *desire* for completeness, or to merge oneself with the other, is the deeper nature of love."

"But Mentor," Maria replied, "I was raised on the proverb 'There is no greater love but that one lay down his life for another' (or something like that). Isn't that sacrificial love?"

"Sacrificial love points to something deeper. One sacrifices oneself for another, because one *desires* the well-being of the other over oneself. Sacrifice emerges from our sense of unity with the other. The more we feel merged with, or united in, the other, the more readily we sacrifice for another. The more distant or objective we feel toward another, the less motivated we are to sacrifice. My joy lies in your joy; my fulfillment lies in your abundant life. In a sense, self-sacrifice is a function of self-affirmation. No, I think the best way to describe this unexpected generosity on the part of the infinite toward the finite is not to say that the infinite *must* care, but that the infinite *wants* to care."

"Mentor, I am Antonia." Each looked at the other in recognition. "You are saying that this *desire* on the part of the infinite toward the finite is what prompts the infinite to reach down even as the finite reaches up. These metaphors are so inadequate, but you know what I mean! Yet, if you will forgive the metaphor, it all sounds more like lovers groping in the dark, when what you really hope for is a lasting, lingering, passionate, committed, total, heart-to-heart embrace."

"I understand what you are trying to say. The experiences of Kairos, Logos, and Mythos lead to a huge diversity and complexity of events, ideas, and relationships—all of which can help us experience the intersection of the infinite and the finite, but none of which is *decisive* in itself. If the centered self escapes us, we long to see or experience the centered self as a genuine hope. That is why, given my background and disposition, I speak of Jesus the Christ—or incarnation. 'Incarnation' is the paradox of the fullness of divinity and the fullness of humanity, united at last. It is visible and mysterious, real and more than real. It is a paradigm that declares 'This is what the truly centered self looks like; this is the possibility of life-at-peace.'"

Maria interrupted, still preoccupied with her particular train of thought. "It's Maria again. How can you welcome the term *Jesus the Christ* as the paradigm for the intersection of the infinite and the finite, when you have just rejected the term *grace* as a means to describe it? I'm confused."

"I am putting words to the experience of incarnation, but I am dissociating the experience of incarnation from any institutional form that pretends to own it. A world of difference separates the experience of Jesus the Christ and the subsequent dogmatic formulas and ritual practices developed by churches to contain it. The entire history of the church—and the predisposition of finitude—is to contain the experience of incarnation in controllable, manageable, data bytes."

He looked out beyond the boardwalk. "It is as if we would siphon off a vial of seawater from this bottomless, limitless ocean and say, 'This is the sea.' The vial of seawater sampled off Crete, the vial of seawater sampled off Japan, the vial of seawater sampled off Australia, and the one off this very beach are all slightly different, prompting us to quarrel about whose vial of seawater truly captures the infinite. I admit I am using the words *Jesus the Christ* and referencing a moment in time that presented Jesus the Christ. I know I might point to other times and use other words. In the end, however, I am not pointing to the vial but to the ocean, and that ocean will shatter every attempt to contain it."

Wally, ever practical, returned our attention to the discipline at hand.

"Ah yes," replied the mentor. "We have this Hope Rosary in our hands, and we have meditated on the ways of being and how we are living them. Now we begin the circuit of the necklace itself. First, we discover ten beads in a row. The first six guide us to reflect on the six experiences of incarnation. As we reflect on the significance of incarnation, we find that we experience incarnation in our own lives through six fundamental ways. These correspond to the six-pointed star graphic. Three are experiences of incarnation as the infinite reaches down—expressions of the *divinity* of Christ, if you will. Three are experiences of incarnation as the finite reaches up—expressions of the humanity of Jesus, if you will. My choice of words is purposeful, but not essential, to help illuminate the experiences of incarnation."

"This is Debra. In other words, incarnation is a single paradigm—the epitome, as it were, of the intersection of the infinite and the finite. We experience it, however, in six fundamental ways, depending on where we are in life. Right?"

Mentor nodded. "Each of the next six beads in the necklace invites you to reflect on a different experience of incarnation. Depending on how you have focused reflection about life-on-the-edge or life-in-between, different experiences of incarnation will be more or less meaningful to you at any given time. Yet incarnations most relevant to you now may lead to incarnations that should, or could, become more relevant to you later—and by understanding these connections, you can give direction to your spiritual journey." He paused to see if everyone understood.

"The first bead evokes reflection on what I call the 'Cosmic Christ.' This is the experience of incarnation that is the most apocalyptic and life-changing. Christ shatters all attempts to define incarnation in dogmas or to contain incarnation in rituals. Christ turns our lives and lifestyles upside down, reshapes relationships, redirects careers, transforms people, precipitates death and birth. The experience of the Cosmic Christ may at times be indistinguishable from evil because it is so painful or seems to be so pointless, but the impact is to change our lives forever. I cannot help but recall images from the ceilings of Orthodox churches. They picture Christ sternly gazing down at everything below: regal, all-powerful, dominant, and even frightening."

"This is the experience of incarnation with which I identify most," Wally said after giving his name. "I am profoundly moved by this kind of setting, and I yearn to break free from the constant trivialities and micromanagement that burdens my professional and private life. I would meet this Christ, if I could."

"I see that you are the kind of person who will remain after we finish today, sitting on the boardwalk, eager to endure the rage of the afternoon thunderstorm that even now we see rumbling on the horizon. You are prepared to put yourself in harm's way if it will connect you with infinite meaning. It may be that other experiences of incarnation will become relevant if you are actually struck by lightning." It was unclear whether or not the mentor was joking.

He continued. "The second bead evokes reflection on the 'Vindicating Christ.' This is the incarnation of justice, judgment, and rescue for the poor, the defenseless, and the victimized. The metaphors describe God as King, Lord, or Messiah; and the hope is both present and future. It is not difficult to imagine this incarnation being powerfully relevant to those being persecuted or enslaved or abused. Their anger is absorbed in God's anger; their vindication lies in some intervention from a Higher Power. The language describing the participation of the infinite and the finite includes references to covenant, obedience, obligation, and duty. I readily think of the ancient prophets who called people, powers, and principalities to repent."

Antonia identified herself. "This is the experience of incarnation with which I identify the most. It's the hope that prompted me to go to law school and work for the district attorney and then begin my own practice for litigation and defense. No matter how frustrated I get with the legal system, this expectation that one day—one day—real justice can replace mere law drives me to continue in my career. Frankly, some days it is so tempting to give up to cynicism and just sell computers." At this final remark, Bill looked quite hurt, and Antonia saw it. "Sorry," she said.

"To some extent the choice of our career may reveal the incarnation we secretly long to experience," Mentor mused. "We are used to thinking of some careers as 'vocations' and others as 'jobs.' Yet a calling lies hidden behind all career choices, each one opening opportunities to experience the incarnation most relevant to our progress in life.

"The third bead evokes reflection on Christ the 'Perfect Human,'" he continued. "In the twentieth century we talked a great deal about what it means to be 'truly human,' but came to no consensus. One presumes it means being reasonable, vulnerable, and authentic; true to oneself, loyal to others, and open to learning new things; or sensitive, strong, and holistically healthy. Yet even those attributes are unclear. Is this the Renaissance Man, the Byronic Hero, the Nietzschean Superman, the Freudian Analyst, the Feminist Advocate, or simply whatever you want to be without any criticism? My reference to the perfect human implies freedom from addiction. Christ, the Perfect Human, is free from any self-destructive behavior pattern.

"Paul complained that 'I do not do the good I want, but the evil I do not want is what I do' [Rom. 7:19, NRSV]. If the predicament of humanity is like that, then the Christ is the only one who is guaranteed to do the good that he chooses and avoid the evil that he rejects, with no ambiguity whatsoever. He is 'human' the way 'humans' are supposed to be: perfectly attuned to the universe, alienated from no thing and no one, the friend of God. He is a microcosm of the way the universe works, subject neither to death, nor corruption, nor pride."

"Remember me? Debra. That, I think, is the experience of incarnation with which I identify the most. It is about being immanently reasonable and utterly ethical. One aspires to it, but never quite achieves it. One teaches it, but never quite learns it. Self-defeating behavior always gets in the way. Education is about shaping people to be 'truly human.'"

A sneering laugh broke the thread of conversation, precipitating a sudden silence. I have said that a number of new people had joined the group on the boardwalk, some invited by previous participants, others who were new to all of us. One of these now erupted: "That is so much bull, that I can't believe my ears! All this stuff about the 'infinite' and the 'finite,' impressively empty words like *Kairos, Logos,* and *Mythos,* and now this bull about being 'truly human,' or righteous judgment, or supernatural acts. I can't believe you are all being taken in by this stuff! Talk about living an illusion. People on drugs have a clearer sense of reality than you people! Life is very simple. It's about the survival of the fittest. The strongest, the smartest, and the luckiest win out over the weakest, the stupidest, and the most unfortunate. They do that as long as they can, until someone better eventually overtakes them. End of life. Period. Everything else you hear is just bull, a conspiracy of religion, science, government, business, and whatever to keep you in your place by promising pie in the sky."

Anger and offense rose up among the participants in the group, but Mentor just smiled, drank coffee, and occasionally even nodded encouragement for the speaker.

"And you are…?" he asked.

"Stop playing games," replied the stranger. "You don't know me, and knowing my name won't mean anything. I'm not interested in shaking hands and being polite. You are all deluded into thinking there is 'something more' to life! It's just a big promotional gambit to protect power, preserve dead institutions, and sell books."

"Well then, for the sake of argument, I shall call you Thor, because the reality you describe sounds very much to the taste of the Viking raiders and reality TV. Let us explore your theory of corporate delusion. We have gathered in just this small group an extraordinary collection of minds across the sectors of public life: doctors, lawyers, business leaders, nonprofit CEOs, educators, and engineers at the top of their professions. They are possessed by no little intuition and intelligence. It is remarkable that all of them, individually and with no prior collusion, have the same intuition that there has to be more to reality than meets the eye."

The stranger (Thor) just scoffed. "You just don't have the guts to admit the truth. The truth is that *there is nothing out there.* What you see is what you get. For all your subtle words and suggestive hints, life is what it is and nothing more. It's just an *ocean* and a *beach,* folks. You play beach ball on the one and avoid sharks in the other. That's it."

"I have no statistics readily at hand, but I think we can conservatively estimate that over the past two millennia several billion people around the world have felt drawn to experiences of the infinite through many religions. In the church alone, we might estimate that over this time nearly one million church leaders have debated, synthesized, and tested the meaning of incarnation. Of them, not a few hated one another's guts and would have done anything to disprove the theology of an adversary or connive in the downfall of a competitor.

"And you are suggesting that throughout that history a grand conspiracy of church leaders sought to conceal the truth that you have finally, after all this time, discovered to be accurate. Is this likely? Occam's razor is an old and simple method to discern truth, which I might paraphrase in this way: In the most complex situations and conundrums, the simplest answer is most likely the truth. Is it simpler to imagine a conspiracy of billions of people over hundreds of years, or to imagine that you are mistaken?"

"But what you are saying is just so much gibberish," replied Thor, unwilling to back down. "This talk about Christ as a cosmic, righteous, perfect reincarnation of Teddy Roosevelt is just too fantastic for words. It is obviously just a salve for the conscience of industrial engineers, lawyers, and overpaid college presidents." Wally, Antonia, and Debra all had fire in their eyes, but the mentor still sat thoughtfully, sipping his coffee. I don't know what he was thinking, but the old saying about "giving someone enough rope" kept going through my uncharitable mind.

Mentor nodded. "Of course, I did not say 'reincarnation,' but 'incarnation,'" he said gently, "and in that distinction there is a world of difference. If the Christ were a *reincarnation,* then we might eventually claim to be gods ourselves, having passed through various stages of perfection. Indeed, we might salve our consciences with the confidence of absolute certainty. Christ as *incarnation* leads to the opposite conclusion. We will never unite with the infinite unless it is through the generosity of the infinite. Generosity begets generosity; and we must make room for the possibility that, however confident we might be about the truth, we are wrong. What I say to interpret the intersection of the finite and the infinite may be gibberish, but you cannot so readily dismiss the intuition that there *is* an intersection between the finite and the infinite."

"It's still bull," Thor replied, unrepentant. "You are all cowards who cannot face facts."

"So we face a decision—you and I. On the one hand, we are cowards who are avoiding reality, while you have the courage to admit the truth. On the other hand, you are the coward who is avoiding his own potential, and we have the courage to risk the unknown. We could argue the point forever without convincing each other. Indeed, is this not the precisely the dilemma we will argue in our own minds as we live on-the-edge and in-between? You simply have to decide. But the very fact that *you have to decide*—that is, you have to take risk, invest yourself one way or the other, commit to what is *really real*—implies that existence is just such an intersection of depth of being and power of being. Perhaps our courage on this side may be met by generosity on the other side. So now, decide. Either seize the courage to walk away, or seize the courage to shut up and listen."

Thor stood with a snort of derision and left, but I noticed he paused at the vendor down the boardwalk and eventually returned to sit in the sand a short distance away. From there he could both watch the girls on the beach and eavesdrop on our conversation. I gathered he had chosen a third option: to simply remain in perpetual indecision. Meanwhile, the group readjusted themselves and turned once again to the mentor. The sun was higher and the breeze had increased, so we had to cluster closer together and seek shade where we could.

"Mentor, can we *please* get on with the explanation of the Hope Rosary? We have only explored three of the six ways we experience incarnation." Wally was speaking. Ever practical.

"Actually, our previous conversation with young Thor is a helpful transition to talk about the experiences of incarnation from the midst of finitude. The skepticism and rather self-centered pragmatism of our day results, I think, from an unending series of broken promises and bad faith. Religion, science, industry, and nations have all promised so much—and have all failed to live up to their promises. Little wonder that people have turned their attention to mere survival and self-advancement. Their elders have betrayed them, and their institutions have broken faith."

The retail vendors were now opening their stalls, trading ribald jokes, and turning on rival music stations. More people gathered on the beach, especially families with young children searching for shells and building sand castles.

"The fourth bead evokes reflection on Jesus the 'Promise Keeper.' This is one who will never let us down, will always be there when we are in need, and will never forsake the beloved. The Promise Keeper is the one who has said he will return and who will return. The Promise Keeper is associated with 'intimate beginnings' because fidelity is the unconditional demand of intimacy. We may fail to be loyal, and we may fail to uphold our commitments; but Jesus is the intimate who will fully live up to our expectations."

"I'm Bill. This is the experience of incarnation with which I most identify. I realize that may seem paradoxical, because in truth I have been the greatest disappointment to three wives and several children for whom they have custody. Intimate beginnings have not flowered into fidelity for me; and, of course, I know that today I am the norm rather than the exception. Anyway, that doesn't mean I don't care. It's just the opposite. I'm actually pretty desperate to experience a God who is better at keeping his word than I am. Maybe if I experienced that incarnation, I would be better at keeping my word. Business really is like life. If I can't maintain a reputation for keeping my promises, I am nothing."

"The fifth bead," the mentor continued, "evokes reflection on Jesus the 'Healer.' The experience of life struggle leaves a trail of broken health, broken minds, broken hearts, and broken dreams. The experience of healing is one of the most powerful ways people connect with the infinite. This can be through, along with, or even in spite of the medical science of our times. Healing is no more miraculous than keeping promises, although it captures the imagination of the public more powerfully."

"Remember? I'm Maria, and I suppose it is no surprise that this is the experience of incarnation with which I most identify. Yet as a surgeon, I confess I both yearn for and doubt this incarnation. Perhaps I have seen too much death or simply know the limitations of medicine all too well.

When I try to go beyond the boundaries of medicine to seek God's aid, more often than not I am disappointed."

The mentor responded. "We see in Jesus the Christ the fullness of the intersection of the infinite and the finite, one result of which is healing. The fundamental healing is the mending of the brokenness between the infinite and the finite—disease and death being the foremost signs of this alienation. The experience of this in daily living remains mysterious. That is to say, life does not *cease* to be a struggle; our need for new beginnings does not cease to be urgent; our questions continue to demand conversation with a spiritual guide. Jesus the Healer must connect with other incarnations as well. Tragedy and ecstasy are really two sides of the same coin. That is the ambiguity of existence. Reflect on the past week of surgery, and you will recall scenes of pathos and scenes of inarticulate joy. Within the pathos, does something 'stand out' with some positive potential? Within joy, does something 'reality check' the most optimistic prognosis?"

Maria smiled slyly. "You are saying to me exactly what you said to Thor, aren't you? You are saying that the incarnation of healing visible in Jesus only exists ambiguously, as long as the finite remains alienated from the infinite. You are saying we can find evidence for both skepticism and hope. You are telling me to have the courage to decide which one I will risk my life and career on."

The mentor smiled slyly in return. "And I am asking you to decide now, right here on the beach, before you go back to work."

He continued. "The sixth bead, and the last of the fundamental incarnations of Jesus the Christ, is the experience of Jesus the 'Spiritual Guide.' You will remember that earlier we distinguished between a spiritual guide (a tactic) and the paradigmatic yearning for a spiritual guide (the incarnation). The point is that the infinite does not leave us without witnesses. Some guides are well known, perhaps associated with religions or philosophies; and some may be ephemeral, providing anonymous insight in emerging crises and then vanishing from our attention. The difficulty is that authentic spiritual guides are more clearly seen in retrospect. That again is the ambiguity of existence."

Calvin had been silent for some time. He, among all of us, had appeared the most despondent and hopeless; but throughout this conversation he had clearly been brightening. "Remember me? Calvin. It is with this experience of incarnation that I most identify. It is simultaneously what I most yearn to have and what I most yearn to become. What I wouldn't give to literally follow Jesus the Christ across the Sea of Galilee, to sit at his feet on just such a beach, and to find help through the ambiguities of daily living!"

Just at that instant, the amusement park opened with a roar of machinery and loud music. The incongruity of Calvin's words and our situation made everyone, even Calvin, laugh. Once the noise faded into the background of our consciousness, both invasive and contained, we were able to focus on the mentor's reply.

"I think the Bible story about feeding the five thousand left out the part about the Ferris wheel. I think that is unfortunate, because it distorts the reality of what it means to experience incarnation as spiritual guidance. Under the conditions of existence, spiritual guidance must compete with so many other distractions and manipulations. How is it to be recognized as more than just another manipulation? Spiritual guidance must lead the disciple back to the other five experiences of incarnation, each of which responds to the fundamentals of life (infinite and intimate beginnings; life struggle and myth-making; reasonable order and intuition)."

"Mentor, the Hope Rosary has ten beads here, and you have only discussed meditation on the six experiences of incarnation. What are the other four beads?" Mentor glanced about the group, searching for the speaker to make eye contact.

"Over here. This is Debra, ever teachable."

"The final four beads in the string of ten focus on mission. It makes meditative sense to move from reflection about the ways in which the infinite behaves generously toward the finite to the ways in which we should behave generously in our daily living. Generosity begets generosity. We have seen six fundamental, incarnational, ways in which the infinite is generous. Now we will look at four basic ways through which we align ourselves with that generosity. Purposeful living is really about alignment. It's about placing oneself within the trajectory of God's generosity and then organizing one's daily living to direct that arrow to the target. We often talk about distractions, sidetracks, or irrelevancies that divert our lives toward matters of relative unimportance. Our lives are not diverted. Our living diverts God's arrow of generosity, causing it to miss the mark."

Antonia chuckled. "I have this image of Cupid's arrow consistently missing because some idiot bumped the target, causing the wrong people to fall in love with the wrong thing."

"Well," replied the mentor, "without reducing the generosity of the infinite to a greeting card, that is not a bad analogy. The *Eros* toward the world, which is the nature of infinite generosity, is really about causing the right people to fall in love with the right thing at the right time. That is the *Kairos* experience—the link between infinite beginnings and intimate beginnings. For that arrow to fly true, we align our personal mission with God's mission. The next bead after the six experiences of incarnation reminds you of God's mission. I often describe that mission as 'the redemption of the world.' Others speak of 'the reality of the realm of God,' but perhaps these terms are too vague or burdened by my Christian upbringing. Perhaps we might say God's mission is 'the reunion of the finite and the infinite,' or 'the convergence of life beyond the conditions of existence.'"

"It seems to me (Calvin) that you are saying God's mission is the permanency of life-at-peace. That is the third way of being that you asked us to delay discussing earlier in our conversation. You said at the time that we could not really talk about life-at-peace until we better understood the generosity of the infinite toward the finite. So you limited us to talking about life-on-the-edge and life-in-between. Now I see why. Life-at-peace becomes clearer to me as the hope of kept promises, healing, and guidance and the balance of reason, meaning, and import. These are the six experiences of incarnation."

"What do you mean by 'import'?" asked someone from the group.

"I mean the intentionality or desire of the infinite to reunite with the finite that is the very essence of Kairos," Calvin replied.

"Yes," said the mentor. "My own mentor used to talk about the purposefulness of this infinite generosity as 'import.' Life-on-the-edge he would have described as radical autonomy, associated with the courage to be oneself. Life-in-between he would have described as radical heteronomy, associated with the courage to be in relationship. Life-at-peace he would have described as radical theonomy, associated with the courage to accept acceptance. He would describe the mission movement to accomplish such a convergence as 'life in the Spirit.'"[1]

"But how do we reflect on aligning ourselves with God's mission? It's me, Maria speaking. I've made up my mind—made a decision—right here on the beach. I want to invest myself in the purposefulness of the infinite toward the finite. Obviously, however, I am not going to simply create Kairos! So what do I do?"

"Once you are clear about God's purpose, the next step in alignment is to become equally clear about the purpose of the church. Of course, I know to whom I am speaking. You were raised in the church, or at least in conversation with the church. You are filled with ambivalence (if not outright suspicion) about the integrity of the church. Think of the church not as an institution of members but as a body of believers. It is the company of people who courageously have committed to the generosity of the infinite. The sole purpose of the church is to 'make disciples.' That is, the purpose of the church is to align people to God's mission, one person at a time. This is not about making converts; it's about inspiring, coaching, and leading acts of courage. It's about persuading, convincing, or exhorting people to dare to say no to absolute skepticism and yes to an ultimate hope. The rest of what we mean by 'church' is mere tactics."

"You are saying that it is important to be a part of a company of true believers, presumably across time and geography. It is important to associate yourself with those who believe in this infinite generosity. It's me, Bill, and I naturally think in terms of multinational corporations."

"I don't mean a corporation. That is too institutional. Think 'movement.' This cross-cultural company is more like a network or movement that may have little in common except commitment to the unity of the finite and the infinite. They share a hope, but not necessarily a doctrine or a polity or an incorporated status."

"Having grown up in the '60s (me, Debra), I can tell you that being a part of a movement is not enough. Corporations will trump movements every time."

"Therefore, the next bead evokes reflection on your *team* mission. You gain clarity about God's mission and the church's mission and now your *team* mission. This is the smaller cohort of intimate colleagues and friends, banded together for mutual mentoring and support, who cooperate together to accomplish a particular strategy within the larger movement.

"For example, I myself am part of a team. Our specific mission purpose is 'to guide leaders for ancient mission in the contemporary world.' This has often included Christian leaders, but not necessarily so. We can help Jewish leaders, Muslim leaders, and leaders from many backgrounds; but the strategic contribution our team makes is to focus on *leaders*. We don't develop programs, create agencies, plant churches, found corporations, or educate the masses. We focus on transforming and aligning leaders. The team mission of everyone here will be different."

"Wally here. How do we find and form that team?"

"Trial and error, experimentation, intentional conversation, searching," answered the mentor. "Yet it is not just random. Your awareness of the principles we have discussed and the discipline of your spiritual lives will cause you to recognize comrades when you meet them. The challenge is not to find them, but to shape the team and hold one another accountable to the mission. That is why I designed the mutual mentoring journal you have read elsewhere. This can be done along with your personal use of the Hope Rosary. Teams require concrete disciplines and serious personal commitment. When they fall apart, the arrow from the infinite is deflected off course."

By now the sun was higher, and the beach hotter and windier. Thor was still there, neither further from nor closer to the group. More people were ambling about the boardwalk, and we had begun to attract attention. Angry glares from the vendors indicated we were taking up space. Curiosity brought bystanders closer because we seemed so engrossed in our conversation. Perhaps our very earnestness was attractive and scary. An adult pulled a curious child away, muttering, "They must be alcoholics, or mentally unstable, or some kind of twelve-step group." At any rate, it was soon time to stop and go to work.

"Only the last of the ten beads remains," Mentor said. "And this perhaps is the most difficult meditation of all. You have sought to clarify God's mission, the church's mission, and the team's mission, but in the end it becomes personal. What is *your* mission?"

"Isn't it rather presumptuous to claim a 'personal mission'?" Wally asked after identifying himself. "Does everyone have to be 'on a mission'? It's not just that it seems hard to imagine every person (child, adult, and senior; the physically and emotionally challenged; the affluent and the homeless) having a personal mission; it also seems to denigrate the vocations of those who do."

"The fact that every person should have a personal mission—a vital purpose in life—does not diminish anyone. Yes, it is crucial for all people, no matter who they are, to clarify that vital purpose. A personal mission is the peculiar way you 'give life away' to others. It is the peculiar form of generosity each person can exercise in alignment with the radical generosity of the infinite to the finite."

"This is Debra. Are you suggesting that a personal mission can be any kind of activity that fulfills your own life, too? A personal mission is basically 'what you are good at'?"

"No. What you are 'good at' is different from your personal mission. Wally is good at applied mathematics and building things, but it is unclear who benefits from this or how quality engineering will give life away to someone else. That is what Wally needs to discern. What is the purpose toward which he can apply his best abilities? Let me say this another way. A personal mission is an experience of absolute urgency. It links an identifiable microculture, a describable benefit, and a personal passion. Your absolute urgency is what you reshape your entire lifestyle to pursue. You stake your financial stability, your relationships, and your very health to achieve it."

"It's Bill speaking. If I understand it right, this is more than passion. It is passion that will bless someone other than oneself. I've been passionate about business all my life, but I can't say that it has directly benefited anyone other than me. I guess you could say the only one I have ever felt absolutely urgent about is me."

"Purpose is something for which you will risk your life. Absolute urgency is something you are willing to risk your life right *now*. Purposefulness has an impatience about it that is crucial to the alignment of one's life with the generosity of the infinite. It is a compulsion or an instinct or a homing beacon for your minute-to-minute spontaneity and week-to-week strategy. It is not necessarily something you can do well, but something you must do now. Absolute urgency is the missing piece in Western European and American culture, and perhaps in all declining cultures since the demise of the Roman Empire. Nobody feels absolutely urgent about anyone or any activity that will bless someone else."

Restlessness was now becoming quite apparent among the group, but it was more than just the pressure of time and the need to go to work. People were stretching their legs, eyeing the joggers on the beach, and looking at the time.

"Ask yourself," continued the mentor, "what you feel restless to accomplish? If you feel the pressure to get to work, what is it about work that is crucial to accomplish—so crucial, in fact, that if you did not rush off to accomplish it, something of absolute urgency would go undone? If you feel a need to stretch your legs and jog down the beach, what destination makes it absolutely urgent that you get there? Or will you just go to work…and then go home? Or will you just run down the beach…and turn around and run back again?

"Maria and I—this is Antonia—are curious to know what your personal mission is? What is it that is so absolutely urgent that you would shape your lifestyle to pursue it?"

The mentor did not even pause for thought, but responded immediately. "My mission," he said, "is to mentor pilgrims in the way of Christ." He paused as we absorbed the implications of this rather ambitious goal. "These are more than words. As you can see, I have given this matter considerable thought and tested this compulsion against real life. It rings 'true' for me every time. I feel absolutely urgent about it."

He glanced at Thor, still sitting some distance away. "It may be that if my young 'Viking' acquaintance pulled a gun and demanded that I recant, my physical cowardice would cause me to do so. Yet as soon as he walked away, that inner compulsion would return with even more force. That is the nature of absolute urgency. Is it something that you discern, or something that discerns you?"

After this, the group broke up, reluctant to leave the boardwalk and beach for any number of reasons. All were quickly lost in the crowd that by now was gathering for their entertainment. I noticed that Wally lingered over another iced tea, apparently waiting for the encroaching thunderstorm to overtake him. The mentor had moved to sit in the sand beside Thor. What they were talking about, I do not know.

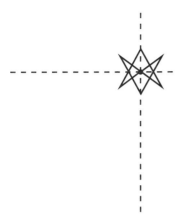

Fourth Dialogue

ECHO'S JOURNAL _

This time our group met at the SportPlex on the outskirts of the city. I was puzzled by the meeting place. The SportPlex is a large facility with three ice rinks, gymnasiums, soccer fields, fitness rooms, and so on. It was difficult to park, crowded, and noisy. The restaurant area was comfortable enough, overlooking the ice rinks on one side and the swimming pool on the other side. However, the coffee was bad, the air reeked of chlorine, and the plastic chairs were hard. Nevertheless, we were all here—and more. I recognized new guests invited by the original core group. Not a few parents lingered within earshot as they waited for their kids to end practice sessions and workouts.

The Teaching

The mentor rarely indulged in a great deal of idle chatter, and today was no exception. With a certain air of urgency, he launched our discussion.

"When we last talked together," he said, "we followed the discipline of the Hope Rosary through the first ten beads on the necklace. The first six beads evoke meditations on the six fundamental experiences of incarnation as expressions of the radical generosity of the infinite towards the finite. The last four beads evoke meditations on aligning ourselves with God's mission."

"Remember me? I'm Antonia. I have been using, and pondering, the discipline of the Hope Rosary. Maria and I have been working together on it. It seems that the movement of meditation takes us from a general conviction that 'the infinite is not neutral to the finite,' to more and more specific intuitions about how the infinite is *generous* toward the finite, and finally how each person may align with that generosity. Yet you teach, and the star graphic implies, that the infinite is also capricious (if I can use that word), or at the very least unpredictable. Kairos can mean disaster as well as blessing. Wouldn't it be possible to logically develop a parallel meditation on *negative* incarnations as well? Expressions of God that are chaotic instead of orderly, for example? or destructive rather than healing?"

The mentor took more than the usual time sipping coffee and thinking about the question. Meanwhile, we watched the sporting tableaus through each window, like gods gazing objectively into three little "universes" of swimming, figure skating, and ice hockey. Some of the athletes were celebrating, and some were crying. Some were winners, and some were losers. Most were so busy just *trying* that they paid little attention to time or target. Finally, he replied.

"I can reply to your question in at least three ways. The first is to say 'I don't know,' but this is not a simple answer. The confession of *not knowing* is usually a more complex answer than the conviction of *knowing*. Is it a psychological trick of being human that leads us to be optimistic about the intentions of the infinite? Or is it a function of the very courage to be that we might anthropomorphically project upon the infinite any intentionality at all? Do we have more to go on than just our gut instinct, blind trust, or arbitrary decision to say that infinite generosity is more basic than infinite animosity? I think we do. Listen carefully, now! I say, 'I *think* we do.' The very ability to *think* about it at all suggests a benevolent connection between the human situation and infinite purpose. If the fundamental stance of the infinite to the finite were one of animosity, the capacity to *think* at all would not serve its purpose. Why be able *to think* at all if the infinite were not generous toward the finite?"

A whistle blew from the pool area, and we turned to see a young boy pulled from the water, spluttering and gasping, after a minor collision with a diver. The coach was volubly explaining with animated gestures. Within minutes the lad was again in the water, learning from his mistake.

After a drink of coffee, the mentor continued. "A second possible response is that good is more likely to come from evil than evil from good. Humans seem to be designed to survive. We are more likely to experience disaster, adapt, and thrive again than to experience success, stop, and die. The same might be said of Darwin's view of nature. Life will find a way."

"This is Maria. Many would say that mere survival does not necessarily mean the perpetuation of what is good. Goodness, beauty, and truth are all relative."

"That depends on your expectations. If goodness were limited to self-interest, beauty to perspective, and truth to sensory data, it might be impossible to leap from survival of the fittest to quest for the good. Why should it be? Why *choose* it to be? Despite intellectual arguments and the persuasiveness of materialism, culture does not *behave* this way. It does not settle with survival, but seeks to *thrive*. The very diversification of forms implies an elusive essence we are trying to capture; the very debate about morality suggests a more profound law we are trying to imitate."

"Sounds like you are making a case for 'progress,'" remarked Maria.

"In a sense," replied Mentor, "but it is not progress based on confidence in human innovation, but confidence based on the lure of the infinite. If there were no such lure, would we seek to thrive? Would we even struggle to survive?"

Sudden excitement in the hockey arena on our left interrupted further conversation. The sounds were muted through the thick glass panes, but one could see the motionless body of a player surrounded by his teammates. Presumably someone had run head first into the boards. Coaches and paramedics rushed out. Fortunately, in a few moments trainers escorted a rather woozy young player to the training room.

"I have a third possible response to your question about positive and negative incarnations of the infinite. Your concern, of course, is that our confidence in the generosity of the infinite toward the finite may be shaken and even turned upside down by experiences of evil. Which is the 'habit,' and which is the 'accident'? The 'habit' of existence is to choose life, health, and relationship, for example, rather than to choose death, disease, and solitude. These latter things happen as 'accident' or as a deliberate departure from the norm. This is why it is so important to align oneself with God's mission and discover that which is absolutely urgent about one's life. The experience of the 'demonic' (the 'incarnation' of evil, as it were) is a distortion, relaxation, or misalignment of absolute urgency. The less clear or less passionate you become in the pursuit of mission, and the less rigorously aligned that mission is with the generosity of the infinite, the more likely God's mission will become neither absolute nor urgent."

"Mentor," interjected Wally, who was clearly impatient with such abstract speculation, "the discipline of the Hope Rosary requires that meditations on the ten beads (the six incarnations of Christ and the four 'checkpoints' to align mission) are actually repeated five times. Why is this repetition necessary?" The mentor stared at him with a questioning expression. "This is Wally."

"Observe the figure skaters practicing their edges on the ice surface," the mentor replied, pointing through the window at the third arena. "See how slowly, carefully, and methodically they balance on one foot and then on the other, carving perfect spirals and figures into the ice—left blade, right blade, first one edge, then another, over and over again. It is both a mental and a physical discipline. It requires both intense concentration (eliminating all the distractions of noise, audience, and mental anxiety) and rigorous training for the muscles of the body (keeping them firm, supple, strong, and naturally molded to accomplish one thing). We can apply the same principle to spiritual meditations. Not just the content, but the process itself is crucial. You may repeat the Hope Rosary without even thinking—by memory—in times of agitation, intense grief, or personal stress. It will still help focus your mind and shape your lifestyle. What the figure skater practices over and over again in relative calm must be performed to perfection in times of enormous stress. Figure skating is a discipline of mind and body; the rosary is a discipline of soul and lifestyle. Repetition is essential."

"This is Calvin. Between each set of ten beads is a single bead. I understand that this bead is intended to elicit a prayer. How do we know what prayer to use? Does it matter?"

"Yes, after each set of ten beads on the necklace is a single bead for prayer. Even in the dark, your fingers can follow the number of beads, prompt your mind for prayer, and focus your mind and lifestyle in any circumstance. I assume that the prayer will be one of the three prayers from the beginning of the Hope Rosary: the Lord's Prayer, the Serenity Prayer, or your personal intercessory prayers. You will know what is appropriate for your life and meditation at that moment. The Lord's Prayer will take you back to the six ways to experience Jesus the Christ; the Serenity Prayer will take you back to the three ways of being in the world; and your intercessory prayers will take you back to the alignment of yourself with God's mission. What is most relevant at any given moment is very personal."

We watched the figure skaters through the glass. Once again I felt godlike, detached from the intense reality in the ice arena on the other side. Perhaps this was one-way viewing glass. What would the skater see from the ice surface on her side of the glass? Would she even suspect that our eyes were watching her? Would she marvel at any connection between her discipline and ours? At times, a skater would falter. A distraction, or momentary inattention, or some unseen bump or groove on the ice would cause her to swerve outside the figure or catch a spike on the blade. Each time she would react with an angry shake of the head or even tears. At times she would step away entirely in despair. Each time the coach would call encouragement, or offer comfort and advice, or even shout in returned anger. Each time the skater returned to the discipline.

The mentor had been observing us observing the skaters. "I see that you understand," he said. "Spiritual discipline is no less intensive than training for competitive sports, business success, law practice, or even the most exacting surgery."

"I'm Bill. I understand the need to master the spiritual discipline—the mental concentration that shapes lifestyle behavior both spontaneously and daringly. Once we trace the Hope Rosary around the necklace, we return to the central medallion. Do we now meditate, finally, on life-at-peace?"

"Yes, exactly. Perhaps you see now why I urged you to focus only on the first two ways of being at the beginning of the meditation process. At first, we concentrate on discerning how our lives are on-the-edge and in-between. That precipitates reflection on the experiences of infinite generosity (incarnations of Jesus the Christ) and on our alignment with God's purpose. Now we can better reflect on the third way of being: life-at-peace. This is both a present possibility and a future yearning."

"Is it *really* a present possibility?" Calvin identified himself. We, who had come to know him over time, could anticipate his deep need for consolation and encouragement after a career in social work.

"Yes! It is a *real* possibility, even in the midst of daily living," replied the mentor with a compassionate smile. "First, the discipline of meditation itself calms the spirit, overcomes despair, and eliminates (if only for a time) the frantic quality of life. You can see this in other disciplines as well—yoga, tai chi, even what are called 'martial' arts. The figure skater, for example, reaches a state in which she is oblivious to the crowd and even of her own self, absorbed by the perfection of the figure and the movement. Time stands still. Similarly, it is possible to experience a convergence of the infinite and the finite in the midst of life (if only for a moment), caused by heightened sensitivity from the spiritually disciplined life and the unpredictable in-breaking, or Kairos, of God's generosity. Those experiences are what we can most truly identify as 'worship.' They are the moments when the infinite is present to the finite and the finite is most alert to the infinite. Radical generosity intersects with perfect gratitude."

"You are not talking about the church or traditional worship services on Sunday morning, are you? This is Debra."

"Not really. I am not saying that traditional worship services *cannot* be experienced as life-at-peace, but that they are *rarely* experienced as such. Worship cannot really be a 'service,' you see. Most worship is a strategically planned, controlled event, primarily designed to convey information or fulfill obligation. Worshipers do not really expect, and do not really want, God to show up. That would upset everything and place intolerable burdens of spiritual discipline on the people. Most people attend worship out of personal need rather than spiritual discipline. What they seek is not life-at-peace, but mere comfort or supernatural magic."

"This is Maria. Isn't that extreme? The Eucharist, for example, ought to be an experience of incarnation in and of itself."

"In this I am simply being practical. A routine of corporate worship is only valuable if it comes from, and leads toward, a routine of personal spiritual discipline. I am not talking about the worship *service* as a function of pastoral care. Comfort is not the same as peace. Worship is a moment of approximation to the infinite, participation in incarnation, alignment of personal destiny and God's mission. That is not something that you can strategically plan into a calendar."

"Then what do you mean by 'life-at-peace'?" Maria asked.

For several minutes we had been watching a dance pair rehearsing on the ice surface in the adjoining arena. The mentor paused thoughtfully to watch them. The muted melody from *The Nutcracker* ballet penetrated the glass window, contrasting sharply with the clatter of chairs scraping, coffee cups clinking, and silverware jangling. In here, all was chaos; out there, all was in order. The pair accelerated into a lift, a spin, legs striding in perfect unison, the man tossing the woman into the air, the woman catching herself on a single blade, arms outstretched, their fingertips touching once again as their blades inscribed the ice in graceful arcs. Perhaps I had become accustomed to the terminology of the mentor. Out there was Logos, expressing Mythos, experiencing Kairos—but in here the chaos showed little purpose and no significance.

"Picture in your minds the star diagram, with the two intersecting triangles of the infinite forming the plane of existence. Life-at-peace is the momentary turn of events that creates simultaneity of infinite and finite experience. It is as if the finite had been turned upside down and inside out, so that there is just *one* triangle. I choose the image of the triangle as the most stable of all foundations, and so life-at-peace is an experience of utter stability that overcomes the passage of time. It is an eternal now."

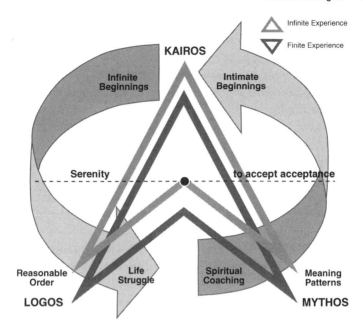

The mentor continued: "In the experience of life-at-peace, life struggle is absorbed into reasonable order; and life is logical, predictable, and manageable again. Spiritual coaching understands the complexity and purpose behind patterns of meaning; and life makes sense, brings fulfillment, and has intrinsic value. Intimate beginnings merge with infinite beginnings, and new life overcomes death; new love overcomes alienation; and new hope overcomes despair. The depth of serenity is the unreserved acceptance of unconditional acceptance. The finite and the infinite reunite."

"If I understand you," said Bill after identifying himself, "the centered self of which you spoke earlier could also be described as the 'serene self.' It is an experience of serenity—a kind of attunement with the infinite?"

"I realize that we are fighting with words, now, to describe an experience 'beyond words.' We should start writing poetry, singing songs, or projecting images to reflect on life-at-peace, rather than converse in words, write essays, or formulate abstractions. I suspect that Thor would be highly amused or very annoyed if he were among us today, because his best approximation of serenity would be 'pleasure.' But yes, you are right. The centered self experiences a serenity, balance, or harmony with the infinite. It may happen by chance or be precipitated through spiritual discipline, but we have no guarantees that we can achieve or control it."

"Wait a minute! This is Calvin. What do you mean we have no guarantees? I thought that if we pursued a serious spiritual discipline, life-at-peace would at least be a reasonable expectation!"

"The more you strive for it, the more it eludes you. The more you allow the spiritual discipline to align you with the generosity of the infinite, the more you concentrate on others rather than yourself, and the more likely peace will find you. Most of us use the term *spiritual discipline* as if it were a noun with an adjective. We think of *discipline* as a subject matter, curriculum, or exercise program that we can manipulate and customize for our needs. Yet the word *discipline* is also a verb. The infinite 'disciplines' us—chastises, teaches, challenges, and exercises us. We are both subject and object. The experience of life-at-peace is influenced, but not controlled, by our actions."

The dance pair had been practicing a single maneuver over and over again, their coach often in animated conversation, although her words were beyond our hearing. This time they accomplished the maneuver, and each dance partner remained motionless on the ice, frozen in the final positions, gazing ecstatically into one another's eyes, lost yet found.

"This is Debra. Could we go back? Some important ideas went by real fast, and I need to catch up. It sounds as if the inner working of life-at-peace (so to speak) is that three dualities come together. It is as if the finite 'reaching up' and the infinite 'reaching down' finally embrace. The first duality that is reconciled is that life struggle is absorbed in reasonable order. Can you explain further?"

"I mean that the chaos and conflict, unpredictability and tortuous routine of life are resolved in Logos. Life becomes understandable and manageable, healthy and harmonious. Life is logical again. It makes sense. We can anticipate the future, appreciate the past, and manage the present. It is no longer a daily competition or struggle for survival. Plato and Augustine understood this in the context of civil order or politics: a perfect city, with responsible magistrates and faithful citizens, in the midst of which God in person is King. It is the 'city of God.' As in the vision of Revelation, there is no crying or pain or competition or abuse or racism or violence in this 'New Jerusalem.'"

"Wally here. I associate the word *serenity* with the Serenity Prayer of Alcoholics Anonymous, so I automatically think about alcoholism. The disease makes life a chaos of struggle, destroying individuals and families alike. The cure (or at least the discipline of sobriety) brings a new stability and reliability to personal and family life. Life becomes reasonably ordered again. I can understand how life struggle could or should merge with reasonable order. Cravings come under control; emotions are tamed; life attains a positive consistency it never had before. But what about the second duality? You say that the finite quest for spiritual coaching is merged with infinite patterns of meaning. What do you mean by that?"

"Your own excellent metaphor points to the answer. The alcoholic (or any addict) usually requires a 'sponsor' or guide to support her on the road to sobriety. This sponsor can help the alcoholic rediscover self-esteem, discern a new purpose, and shape new and healthy habits of behavior. My point is that life-at-peace implies a new, overarching 'myth' that gives meaning and purpose to life. In this myth everyone participates and can be a guide to everyone else. Consider the eras of greatest peace and harmony in history (ancient Egypt, the golden age of Athens, second-century Rome, eighth-century China, the High Middle Ages in Europe, the late nineteenth century in America, for example). Every occasion had its own universal myth, or pattern of meaning, in which all could participate."

"The most difficult duality for me to grasp (Debra speaking again) is the third. You say that intimate beginnings and infinite beginnings become the same thing. What do you mean? How can this be?"

"I mean that intimacy and ecstasy become interchangeable experiences. Each one leads to the other. Even the smallest new beginnings in existence reveal clearly an infinite import. Our initiatives are perfectly aligned with God's will; God's will is perfectly expressed through our actions. The depth of being (our human willfulness) and the power of being (God's generous providence) are attuned to each other. Because we have been using both personal and corporate examples, let me try to use them again. The recovering alcoholic experiences every new breath and every new day as a gift from God and feels compelled to pass that hope on to other addicts. Conversely, every new breath and every new day evokes from the recovering alcoholic a determination to align even the simplest and smallest activities to this larger purpose of health and hope."

"Let me offer a corporate example," Calvin said after identifying himself. "Culture itself, in all of its technological and artistic innovation, would become perfectly transparent to the infinite. That is to say, the pursuit of the Good, the Beautiful, and the True, which culture has at best approximated and at worst destroyed, is now fulfilled. It would be as if the Kairos 'moment' became a Kairos 'eternity.' Culture and Spirit would be synchronized." Calvin looked particularly pleased with this hopeful insight.

A great clamor of voices and hockey sticks interrupted us. The door to the other arena opened to let in a troop of children so encumbered by pads, jerseys, helmets, and hockey sticks that you could not tell them apart except for their numbers. They could not have been more than eight years old, all yelling and cheering and tripping over themselves on the way to learning what it meant to "be a team."

"Antonia, here. Both your examples and this discussion lead me to think that life-at-peace is both a present possibility and a future hope. Neither is controllable or predictable, but perhaps influenced and anticipated. Correct?"

"Yes, I think we are driven to see it that way. The conviction that the infinite is fundamentally generous toward the finite leads us to the confidence that this generosity has a point. The reunion of the finite and the infinite is both now and yet to come. The real point of the entire exercise is to renew hope. That is why I have described this talisman as the 'Hope Rosary,' distinguishing it from the ancient one. The former rosary was really about maintaining orthodox faith and finding comfort in adversity. It was most effective as a tool of Christendom for Christendom. The Hope Rosary is designed for 'God Fearers" living in a pagan world. You might say that the Hope Rosary is not a gift from the church to a catechumen joining the institution, but a gift from an apostle to a pagan. It represents the only serious alternative to the noble struggle and self-determined suicide advocated by Marcus Aurelius and the Stoics' tradition from Athens."

"So how do we complete the exercise? We have followed the beads from cross pendant to central medallion, and then around the necklace in five repetitive cycles back to the medallion again. I don't know about anyone else, but I find that the process may take me as little as ten minutes. By the time I'm back to the central medallion, I already feel more calm, focused, and, well, peaceful. What next?"

"Complete the discipline following the beads back to the pendant. It is simply the reverse order of how you began. Yet I suspect that the spirit in which you undertake the 'return trip' will be different from the spirit in which you began the discipline. You began under stress; you return in peace. You began in doubt; you return in faith. You began in anxiety, and you return with courage. So, touch the single bead below the medallion, and repeat the 'Fear not' scripture from Isaiah. This time it is less a statement of defiance against chaos and more an affirmation of confidence in the midst of Chronos.

"In other words (this is Bill speaking) the discipline of the Hope Rosary has helped. It has calmed and focused our thoughts. We are able to think long term and see something beyond the routine of life and the succession of fleeting moments." Clearly, Bill was not really asking a question, but speaking aloud his own conclusion.

"Next," continued the mentor, "offer further intercessory prayer, repeat the Serenity Prayer, and then follow with the Lord's Prayer. All these prayers will have a new character of thanksgiving. You will utter less plea and more expectation. You will have not only a better idea what you are asking, but a clearer idea of what you are seeking."

During these words I noticed someone familiar exiting the changing room connected to the pool. Thor was carrying his gym bag and towel. It suddenly made sense why we had first encountered him at the beach. I was struck by the extraordinary coincidence that we should meet again here. I doubted that he had seen us; but after he bought coffee at the bar, he seemed to linger at the glass watching the swimmers in the pool.

The mentor continued talking. "Recite the Apostles' Creed once again, touching the next single bead. Now, once again, you hold the jagged edges of the cross pendant. I customarily remember the simple Chalcedonian Confession, as I did at the beginning, and remember the words of institution of the Eucharist from my childhood: "Take, eat, this is my blood, shed for you; eat this in remembrance that Christ died for you, and feed on him in your heart with thanksgiving.""

"It begins in incarnation and ends in incarnation," murmured Antonia. "It is as if you enter through a portal and exit through a portal, having lived for a time in a place that intersects with the infinite. Even if you see it from a distance, through a glass pane into another reality, you have caught something of the music, the aroma, or the movement of the infinite." Again, it was not really a question. Many of us looked around, sniffed the air, with newly thoughtful expressions.

"Mentor, this is Debra. Is the Hope Rosary a fixed discipline? I mean, can it be customized by the individual. For example, does one have to use the 'Fear not' passage from the prophets, or could you use some other poignant passage from another source?"

Mentor replied, "The power of the meditative discipline is that it *must* be customized by the individual. This is one reason why I urge you to put the star diagram on your computer or PDA and then insert various images in the background that help you enter the portal to experience the infinite. Your images—your passages, your sources—will be different from mine and from one another's."

"This is Maria. Can we also substitute other creeds for the Apostles' Creed? Or use other affirmations than the Chalcedonian Confession? Or even other references than 'Jesus the Christ'?"

The mentor paused to collect his thoughts, and then spoke with great deliberation. "I think so. Yes, because other religions and philosophies focus on the intersection of the infinite and the finite. However, I am also cautious. Not all religions and philosophies are about the reunion of the finite and the infinite. They may have more to do with keeping these separate, manipulating the infinite for finite purposes, or manipulating the finite for infinite purposes. Spiritual dualism, at root, is a denial of incarnation. Among all the possibilities, I believe, Christian experience and reflection has focused more clearly on the incarnation, and has explored more deeply the paradox and significance of incarnation, than any other religious or philosophical tradition. This is what attracted ancient philosophers such as Origen away from the sophisticated theologies of Egypt, and it is what attracts contemporary thinkers like yourselves away from the many religious and cultic options today. The experience of Jesus the Christ opens the power and depth of being."

ECHO'S JOURNAL _

Our time was over. A new crowd was casting envious looks at the chairs we were occupying in front of the windows to the arenas. We quickly agreed on another time and location to gather, not knowing what topic we might discuss, but confident that the time would be well spent. Our group exited, some singly and some with companions in intense conversation. I looked back to see the mentor step up beside Thor with a fresh coffee cup in hand. They stood side by side, watching the swimmers in the pool. I wonder what they talked about.

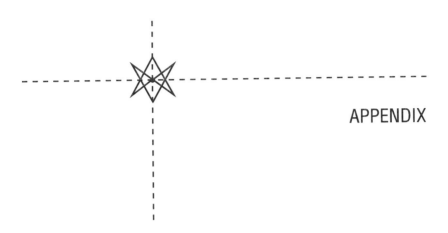

The Ancient Spirituality of "Pilgrimage"

A Monastic Discipline of Talisman Meditation

Journaling has been a significant spiritual discipline since ancient times. The earliest letters of the apostles, apologetic treatises by Christian leaders, analogical commentaries on scripture, and even the *Confessions* of Saint Augustine can all be seen as mature forms of journaling. Reformers and missionaries, such as Martin Luther and John Wesley, and revivalists of the nineteenth and early twentieth centuries also kept journals as a discipline to interface prayer, biblical reflection, historic Christian teaching, conversation with culture, and their ongoing experiences with the Spirit.

Journaling as practiced in the second half of the twentieth century, however, is a mere shadow of the spiritual discipline of the past. For one thing, it has followed contemporary culture by becoming an expression of personal piety rather than community coaching. It has commonly been limited to reflection on a single verse, an inspirational comment, a prayer written by someone personally unacquainted with the reader. It has been kept privately in diary form, never to be shared with another. For another thing, it has followed classic Christendom by organizing reflection around the Christian calendar and Common Lectionary, usually assuming that Christians have predictable agendas that enable them to journal on a daily basis.

Ancient journaling included elements that made the discipline much more profound, with greater impact on mission in a pagan world.

- Journaling was associated with images, symbols, movements, or objects of devotion, including prayer beads, stages of the cross, icons, and pictures. These not only focused meditation, but as visible images and actions, they invited comment from others and encouraged the conversation and sharing so essential to the spiritual discipline.
- Journaling emerged from, and led toward, a more mystical sense of worship that centered on the awesome intersection of the infinite and the finite. The immediacy of God and the companionship with God on the pilgrim journey were part of the same mystery. Worship aimed at the head only motivated people to go to midweek study groups. Worship aimed at the heart motivated people to endure the pilgrim path.
- Journaling as a triad, pilgrimage companionship, or other partnership of like-hearted colleagues was crucial to hold Christians accountable for their discipline and to mutually mentor Christians through the ethical ambiguities and spiritual mysteries of the pagan world.
- Journaling was organized around mission activity rather than ecclesiastical passivity as a way of reflecting aloud about the questions, issues, challenges, confrontations, and disputes that surrounded the beneficial service and faith witness of the Christian movement.
- Journaling was inserted flexibly into a very active and unpredictable lifestyle, in which letters to others or oneself were begun, developed, and finished "on the fly," sometimes over a period of a week or even months.

The journaling discipline described here is both easier and more difficult than many current strategies. It is easier in the sense that it does not assume that participants will rigorously adhere to a repetitive, daily habit and that participants must have profound insights merely by praying religiously and thinking deeply alone in the privacy of their study. Most people who try modern journaling end up feeling inadequate or spiritually shallow. On the other hand, this discipline is much harder because it assumes a philosophical framework quite familiar to the typical education of ancient Christians, but quite unfamiliar to the typical public education of North Americans raised in the scientific empiricism of the late twentieth century. To succeed, this journaling demands serious thought and aggressive conversation.

Ancient journaling for the pilgrim journey was oriented around images, devotional objects, and sound bytes. Most pilgrims could not read. Therefore, they glimpsed the infinite in daily life and then talked about it in stories, linked it to biblical analogies, carved images in stone and wood, and focused their meditation on symbols. Occasionally, they might sing a memorized psalm or remembered liturgical response. Museums are filled with these devotional objects. Cathedrals contained countless carvings and alcoves for meditation. The hostels and way stations of the major pilgrimage roads contained images and artifacts that inspired and encouraged the inward and onward journey. These are not superficial trinkets, nor are they demonic idols. They are talismans.

A talisman is a "global positioning system" for the soul. It is both symbol and portal. It reminds, educates, and explains, but it also conveys a deeper meaning, inspires a greater purpose, and elicits dramatic change. It is more than illumination. It is a sign of hope. It is a method of aligning oneself with God and experiencing the encouragement of God.

To use the "pilgrim journal," the individual must have a talisman. It may be a digital image that can be used as a background behind the star graphic used to describe the intersection of the infinite and the finite.

The pilgrim journal is nothing less than your own imitation of Luke's journal. The Acts of the Apostles is Luke's journal, written as he traveled with Paul and the pilgrim band. That is why he frequently speaks in the first person. It is a *personal* journal, not an objective history. It is his life experience *this week* as he has come to understand its flow and meaning.

Traditional journaling has been a private, daily activity that usually involves a book or curriculum and which usually results in passive self-understanding. The pilgrim journal is very different from traditional, modern journaling processes you might have known:

- The pilgrim journal is done as a companionship. It is completed, discussed, and shared as a small group. It is used for mutual critique and support.
- The pilgrim journal is a weekly activity, face-to-face and/or online, that reflects on the ebb and flow of an entire week of companionship with Jesus the Christ.
- The pilgrim journal involves a graphic image and a devotional object, which is the focus of meditation and a global positioning device for the soul.
- The pilgrim journal emerges from, and leads toward, worship as a mystical experience of the real presence of God.
- The pilgrim journal emerges from, and leads toward, outreach. It is about positioning yourself in God's mission or being used by God as a blessing for others.

The pilgrim journal is intended as a "thinking Christian's journal." It imitates Paul's ability to engage in philosophical and artistic reflection with the popular culture of Athens. It challenges those Christians who have grown up in the post–liberal arts world of mere professional training to recover a more profound vocabulary to talk about spiritual things.

When you use this journaling resource, I encourage you *not* to think of yourselves as a modern discussion group or prayer team taking time out for coffee, Bible study, and conversation. Instead, I encourage you to imagine yourselves as pre-modern pilgrims from Chaucer's time and the ancient world. Committed to a journey of genuine personal risk, you are holding your talismans before you, reflecting on spirit and culture, mutually mentoring one another on the road, and all the while looking for unpredicted opportunities to give life away like "alms to the poor."

Humilitas

Ancient humility is a profound awareness of the real presence of God and radical obedience to the will of God. This surrender to mystery has little to do with psychological self-deprecation and nothing to do with low self-esteem. In fact, surrender to the mystical intersection of the infinite and the finite fills the individual with a sense of self-worth never known before. The sense of awe is the real motivation for long-term perseverance in any spiritual discipline, and that sense of awe needs to be renewed or refreshed regularly.

Step 1–Talisman. Each individual in the pilgrim band shares the talisman, which is both symbol and portal for the intersection of the individual's life and the infinite. This may be a digital image used as background to the star graphic; or an image, object, or sound byte that has seized the individual as a vital connection with God. The talisman will change over time, and that time may be measured in days, weeks, or years. The pilgrim band meditates silently on these talismans, seeking to sense the ancient awe revealed through them. If you are using the Hope Rosary, the members of the pilgrim band may follow the discipline together, silently or aloud. You may pause to focus on the particular relevance of a bead or meditation

Step 2— Worship. The companionship of the pilgrim band worships together. Worship involves no sacred "tactics." It is better if the companionship is equally traditional and radically innovative. Ancient or postmodern practices are better than the modern (i.e., seventeenth–twentieth-century tactics). The only "good worship" is that through which people experience intimacy with God and ecstasy in God's mission.

Step 3—Scripture. The companionship shares aloud a passage, story, or memory of scripture. This may be random or as part of a lectionary. I often connect the meditation with the "Seeker Cycle" of the "Uncommon Lectionary" I have published elsewhere.[1] You might also refer to the stories of the gospel and early church mission from Luke–Acts.

Humilitas is the ability to adapt oneself to new and even uncomfortable roles in life for the sake of God and God's mission. Humility, therefore, leads individuals to explore, experiment, and risk themselves in new insights and behavior patterns for the sake of God.

Conversatio

Conversatio is an ongoing conversation with God. The ancient word for true conversation or serious dialogue was later applied in medieval times to describe the manner of life of the monastery. It described conversation between brothers and sisters of the monastery and their mentor abbot or abbess. It also described conversation among the brothers and sisters themselves as they mutually coached, critiqued, and supported one another in the spiritual life. The emergence of the Seven Deadly Sins or Seven Lively Virtues, for example, was a simple tool for this dialogue to take place. The *conversatio* in the pilgrim journal is based on the star graphic as a global positioning device for the soul and answers three fundamental questions:

Step 1—Where am I? This is the first question we ask as we are lost in the world of speed, flux, and blur. We need to "find ourselves," for better or worse, and define our position in the universe.

Life-on-the-edge has three forms. Everyone in the pilgrim band reflects on life as it has been lived that week to discern the apposition of their lives in proximity or distance from the points of the star. Life as "on-the-edge" may take different turns, or wax and wane, as time passes through the year.

Life-in-between has three forms. Everyone in the pilgrim band reflects on life as it has been lived that week to discern the juxtaposition of their lives between the Kairos, Logos, and Mythos of their lives. As time passes through the year, life as "in-between" may take different turns and experience different struggles and growth spurts.

Life-at-peace has only one form. The fullness of peace may be rare, but each individual reflects on life as it has experienced such serenity this week. This experience may be fleeting or enduring. (Note that this is a true conversation. Individuals both examine their own lives and critique or reality test the lives of their companions. *Conversatio* is both affirming and often challenging to the companions of the pilgrim band.) If you are using the Hope Rosary, the members of the pilgrim band will use the central medallion as a method to reflect on their distance from, or proximity to, the incarnation. It is a way to discern how centered one's life really is.

Step 2—Where did God go? This is the second question we ask when we feel the alienation of existence. We search for God present in our lives, wherever our living has taken us.

Refer to the star graphic to reflect on the six experiences of incarnation. This is the experience of Jesus the Christ. The penetration of the infinite into the finite reveals the Cosmic Christ, the Vindicating Christ, and Christ the Perfect Human. The yearning of the finite for the infinite reveals Jesus the Promise Keeper, the Healer, and the Spiritual Guide. Each individual in the companionship reflects on which incarnation is most relevant to his or her experience at the present moment. If you are using the Hope Rosary, the members of the pilgrim band can refer to the first six beads of each decade. It is a way to focus thought and conversation on each experience of incarnation.

Step 3—Where will we go next? This is the third question we ask when we try to anticipate the immediate future of personal growth. We look for leverage points or strategies to grow into the future. Conversation focuses on three themes:

- *Courage.* All three aspects of existential courage are discussed: the courage to be in relationship, the courage to be oneself, and the courage to accept acceptance. Look to the appositions for clues to the future.

- *Wisdom.* Reflect on the ability to penetrate ambiguity, measure risk, and test options. Look to the juxtapositions for clues to the future.

- *Serenity:* Reflect on the experience of peace and the temptations of harmony, and anticipate the disturbing influence of the next Kairos moment. Reflect on the experience of Christ that you most need to help you in your spiritual journey.

Week to week the conversation will go in many different directions. Some aspects of living, existential attitudes, and experiences of Christ may be more or less important. Each individual should keep a journal of insights. This will allow one to both measure the cumulative growth over the years and anticipate life changes.

Humanitas

The ancient word *humanitas* can be applied to "humanitarian behavior," but it also implies clarity about mission and the ability to rigorously discipline one's lifestyle to give the stranger first place in one's attention. Ancient monastic rules encouraged vows of chastity (giving no offense to the helpless), poverty (removing any temptation to steal), fidelity (focusing true friendship and duty), and moderation (protecting from any excess or self-indulgence). Fundamentally, *humanitas* is about rigorous mission, self-discipline, and compassion for strangers. There are three fundamental questions:

Step 1—Who will go with us? The pilgrim band looks beyond itself to search for the individual mentors, organizational partners, group alliances, and growth processes that can encourage their spiritual growth and take them further toward the mission that is their destination

Step 2—What will we give away? The pilgrim band focuses radical generosity, giving away without price or obligation something that will bless the stranger. It may be an idea, a hope, or an insight; or a word, a message, or advice; or an object, a contribution, or a service.

Step 3—What will it cost us to follow? The pilgrim band decides what price they are willing to pay in changed attitude, heritage, relationship, personal habit, financial stability, or personal security to give life away to a stranger.

If you are using the Hope Rosary, the members of the pilgrim band will find it helpful to use the last four beads of each decade. Reflect on the alignment of personal mission with God's mission and what changes in lifestyle are necessary to bring oneself into closer alignment with God's purpose.

It is important to understand that this spiritual discipline is a constantly repeating cycle. *Humilitas* leads to *conversatio,* which leads to *humanitas.* And *humanitas* leads back to *humilitas.* Compassion in the world always leads to a renewed experience of the intersection of the infinite and the finite and, therefore, to a renewed awe before the mystery of God.

The exercise that follows provides a template that can be used to guide the discipline of the pilgrim band. It is easily adapted for digital hardware (computers and PDAs), so that images and sound bytes can be added to the journal as talismans come and go. The benefit of the discipline is cumulative. If the pilgrim band meets weekly (as a cell group or mission team), this discipline can become a part of their routine. Entries can be compared from year to year. If the pilgrim band functions as a worship design team, the discipline can connect to the lectionary or preaching strategy of the church. Individuals should digitally cut and paste the five pages of the pilgrim journal for their computer or PDA file.

The pilgrim journal is also designed to interface with the portable, personal discipline of the Hope Rosary. If the pilgrim band meets on a weekly basis, this contemporary adaptation of an ancient pilgrim practice can be used portably at any time or place during the week.

The Pilgrim Journal

HUMILITAS: *Awesome Intersection with the Infinite*

Talisman—The image, object, or sound that reminds you of grace and opens you to God.

Worship—The prayer, meditation, or music that celebrates grace and centers you on God.

Scripture—The scripture, story, or living word that interprets grace and focuses your thoughts on God.

CONVERSATIO: *Mutual Reflection and Critique*

Where am I?
Life-on-the-Edge, Life-in-Between, and Life-at-Peace

Where did God go?
The Six Experiences of Incarnation

Where will we go next?
Apposition (Courage), Juxtaposition (Wisdom), and Unity (Serenity)

HUMANITAS: *Compassion for Strangers*

Who will go with us?
Partners, Alliances, and Mentors

What will we give away?
Mission, Generosity, and Hope

What will it cost us to follow?
Sacrifice, Self-discipline, and Perseverance

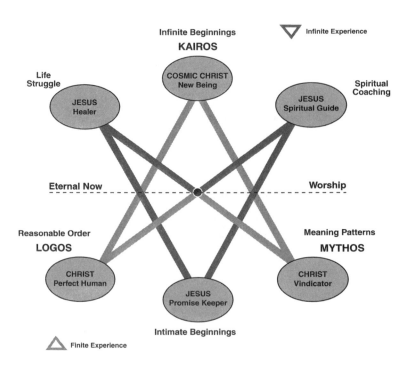

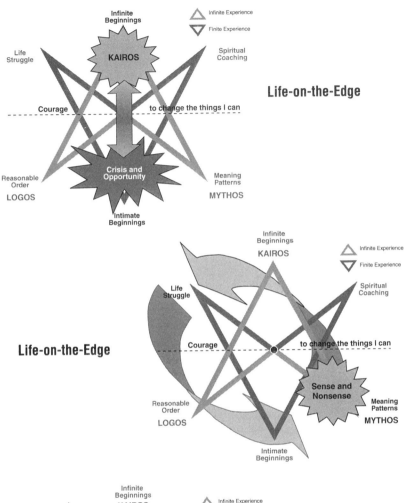

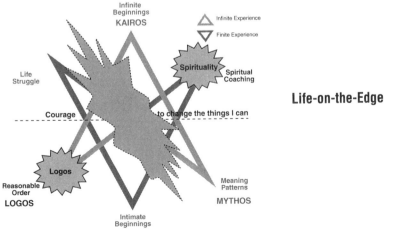

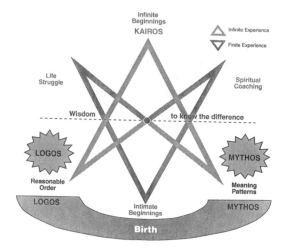

Life-in-Between

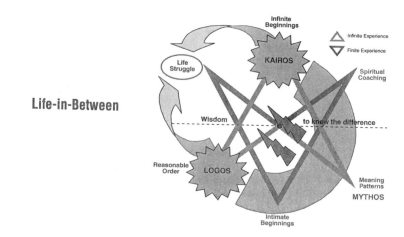

Life-in-Between

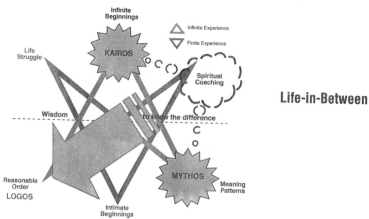

Life-in-Between

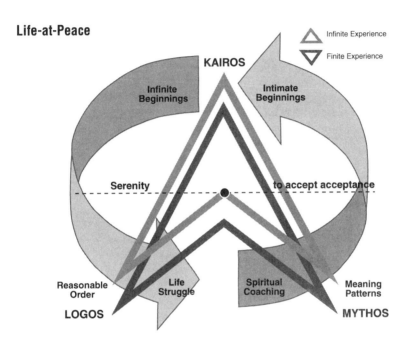

The Hope Rosary
(as explained on pp. 100–102)

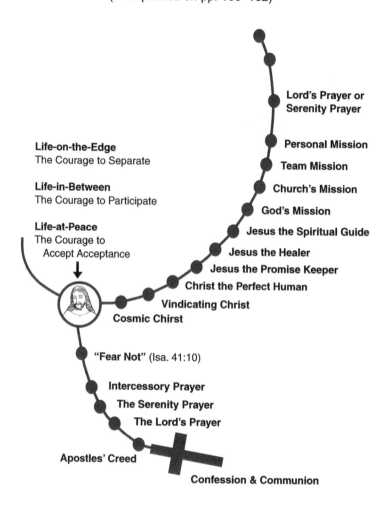

Lord's Prayer or
Serenity Prayer

Personal Mission

Team Mission

Church's Mission

God's Mission

Jesus the Spiritual Guide

Jesus the Healer

Jesus the Promise Keeper

Christ the Perfect Human

Vindicating Christ

Cosmic Chirst

Life-on-the-Edge
The Courage to Separate

Life-in-Between
The Courage to Participate

Life-at-Peace
The Courage to
    Accept Acceptance

"Fear Not" (Isa. 41:10)

Intercessory Prayer

The Serenity Prayer

The Lord's Prayer

Apostles' Creed

Confession & Communion

Notes

Third Mentoring Moment: The Once and Future Quest

[1]Paul Tillich, *Systematic Theology,* 3 vols. (Chicago: University of Chicago Press, 1951), 1: 80, 105 and 3:88.

[2]Paul Tillich, *The Courage to Be* (New Haven, Conn.: Yale University Press, 1952), 86–186.

[3]Paul Tillich, "Kairos," in *The Protestant Era,* trans. James Luther Adams (Chicago: University of Chicago Press, 1948), 32–51.

Fourth Mentoring Moment: Discerning Your Position in Life with Infinite Perspective

[1]Paul Tillich, *The Courage to Be* (New Haven, Conn.: Yale University Press, 1952), 32–63.

Fifth Mentoring Moment: The Experience of Christ

[1]William M. Easum and Thomas G. Bandy, *Growing Spiritual Redwoods* (Nashville: Abingdon Press, 1997).

[2]Paul Tillich, *Systematic Theology,* vol. 2 (Chicago: University of Chicago Press, 1957).

Ninth Mentoring Moment: Life in the Spirit

[1]Paul Tillich, *Systematic Theology,* vol. 3 (Chicago: University of Chicago Press, 1963).

[2]Ibid., 245–75,

[3]Richard Alkerton, in Jonathan Sumption, *Pilgrimage: An Image of Mediaeval Religion* (Totowa, N.J.: Rowman and Littlefield, 1975), 168.

Tenth Mentoring Moment: Where Am I?'

[1]Paul Tillich, *Systematic Theology,* vol. 3 (Chicago: University of Chicago Press, 1963).

First Dialogue

[1]The origins of the Serenity Prayer have been much debated. The present version is reasonably attributed to Reinhold Niebuhr, composed in 1926. See *The Serenity Prayer: Faith and Politics in Times of Peace and War* by Elisabeth Sifton (New York: W.W. Norton, 2003). Some link the prayer to the eighteenth century (Friedrich Oetinger), and others to the sixth century (Boethius). The prayer provided here is similar to that attributed to Reinhold Niebuhr. See http://www.recoveryresources.org/serenity.html.

Third Dialogue

[1]See Paul Tillich, *The Courage to Be* (New Haven, Conn.: Yale University Press, 1952) and also *Systematic Theology,* vol. 3 (Chicago: University of Chicago Press, 1963).

Appendix: The Ancient Spirituality of "Pilgrimage"

[1]See *Introducing the Uncommon Lectionary: Opening the Bible for Seekers and Disciples* by Tom Bandy (Nashville: Abingdon Press, 2006).